Bobby J. Jones

# New Mexico Dreamscapes IV

Bobby  J. Jones

Bobby J. Jones

ISBN:1720702535
ISBN-13:9781720702535

Bobby J. Jones

# DEDICATION

I dedicate New Mexico Dreamscapes IV and its lovely images to my paternal grandmother Bonnie Thelma Turcotte Jones

# Contents

# ACKNOWLEDGMENTS

In New Mexico Dreamscapes IV, I acknowledge the loving memory of my paternal grandmother Bonnie Thelma Turcotte Jones (1903-1982).

My paternal grandmother Bonnie Thelma Turcotte Jones was born on January 26, 1903 in Miami, Roberts County, Texas. She was the youngest daughter of nine siblings, three sons and six daughters.

Her parents were George Cazimyr Turcotte of Trois Rivieres, Champlain, Quebec, Canada and Carrie Amanda Wiant of Nemaha County, Kansas. Her father George owned a ranch near Mobeetie, Wheeler County, Texas.

Her mother Carrie served as the county's midwife. There were no doctors available in the area to care for the citizens in this area of Texas during The Ranching Pioneer Era in The Panhandle.

Seven days after my grandmother's birth, my great grandmother passed away from the influenza that had spread throughout Wheeler County that winter. My grandmother was raised by two foster families in the area. The second foster family, who raised my grandmother, moved to Wichita, Kansas.

Thelma graduated from Wichita High School in 1921. While attending high school, she enrolled in accelerated courses that allowed her to gain college credits at McPherson College. The college during this time was a teacher's college where my grandmother met my grandfather John Herman Jones at a spring dance in 1919. My grandparents fell in love and married on May 28, 1921 in McPherson, Kansas at the home of Dr. and Mrs. John W. Deeter. Dr. Deeter taught Theology at McPherson while Mrs. Deeter taught Art.

During this time in my paternal grandmother's life, she lived with her second oldest brother John and his family in Pampa, Gray County, Texas. After my grandparents were married, my grandfather graduated from McPherson College in 1921 with a degree in Education. According to my grandparents' love letters to each other during their two year courtship, their first teaching assignment was teaching first grade in Springer, Colfax County, New Mexico for the 1921-22 school year.

In 1925, my grandparents moved to Admire, Lyon County, Kansas. Before this assignment my grandparents graduated from McPherson. My grandfather received his second degree in Agriculture; my grandmother received her degree in Education.

My grandparents became parents on October 18, 1928 when their daughter Margaret J. Jones Kennedy was born in Manhattan, Riley County, Kansas. When the Great Depression arrived, my grandparents moved to Pampa, Gray County, Texas in 1930. My dad Herman Anthony 'Toney" Jones was born on September 7, 1932.

By this time, my grandmother had stopped teaching and was raising her children. My grandfather started teaching in the Pampa Independent School District in 1930. According to my aunt, her mom started selling magazine subscriptions to help with family finances.

In 1938, my grandfather graduated from West Texas State College in Canyon, Texas with a M.A. in Education Administration. He was promoted to Assistant Principal at Pampa Junior High School and retired from this school district in 1964. During WW II, my grandmother worked for Pantex on the assembly line to make ammunitions.

My grandparents were very much involved with the Pampa community and their church, First United Methodist Church. My grandparents moved from East Craven Avenue to 601 North Gray Avenue in 1942. This house is what I remember the most from my childhood. I remember the solid, dark wood doors, the wooden baseboards, the crown molding around the doors, the high ceilings, and the glass door knobs. My grandparents were married for 54 years until my grandfather's death in 1975.

My grandmother loved being a grandmother to six grandchildren, four granddaughters and two grandsons. I remember her brownies, her homemade prune cakes, and her corn chowder. I loved playing in her backyard in Pampa on the big swing and the teeter totter that my grandfather built.

On June 22, 1982, Thelma passed away from the complications of cancer in Fort

Worth, Tarrant County, Texas and is buried in Pampa, Gray County, Texas.

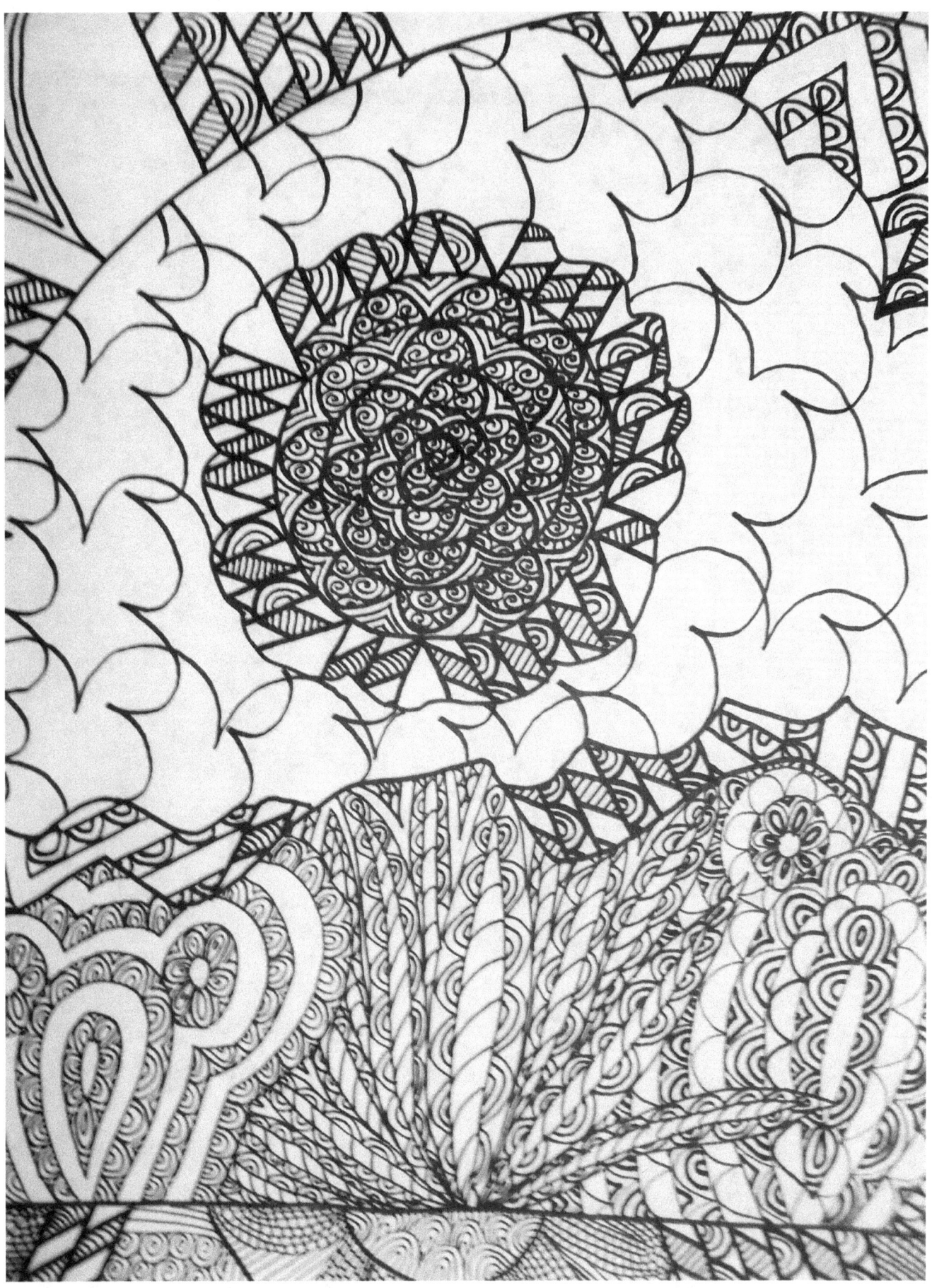

Bobby J. Jones

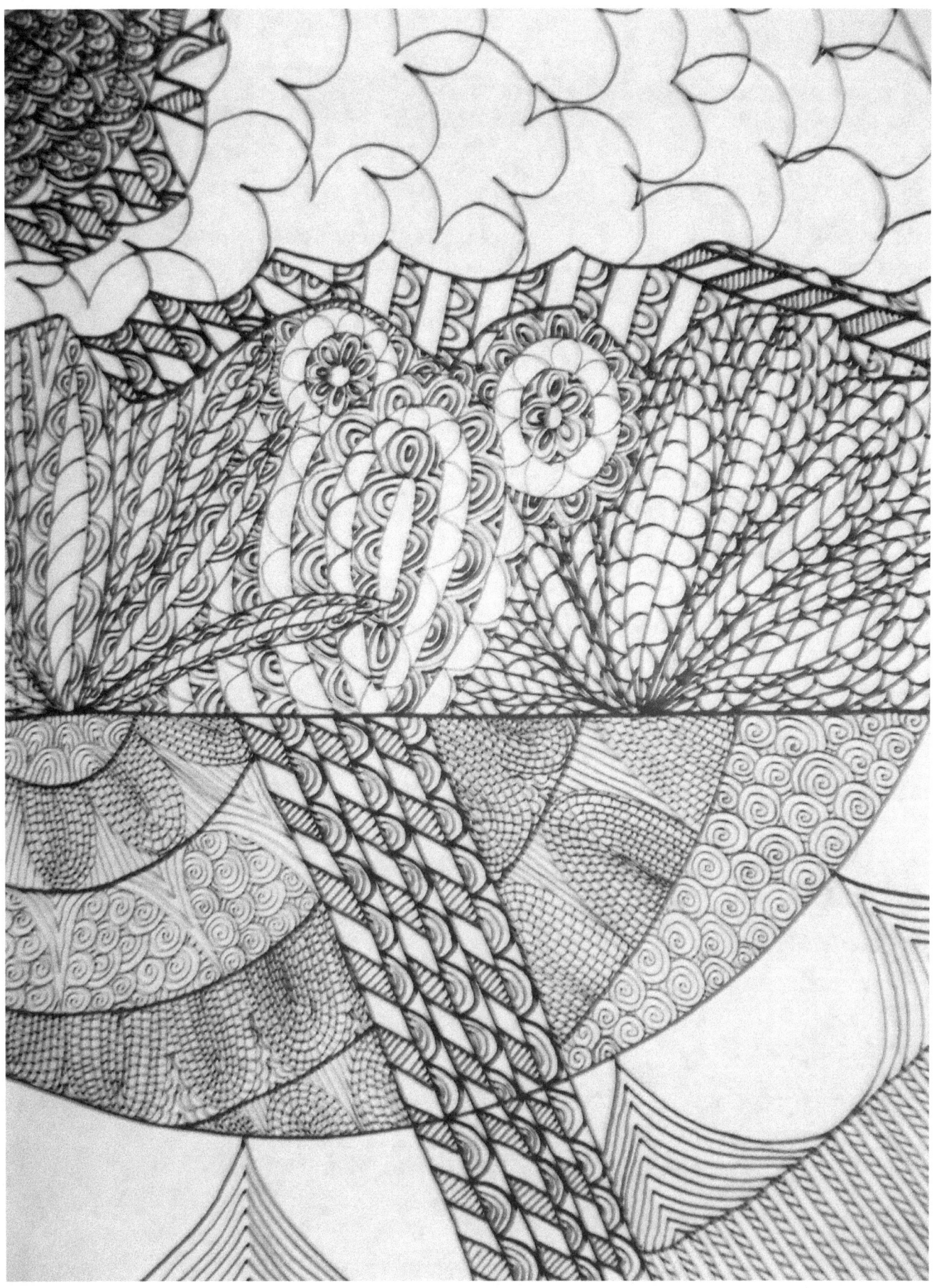

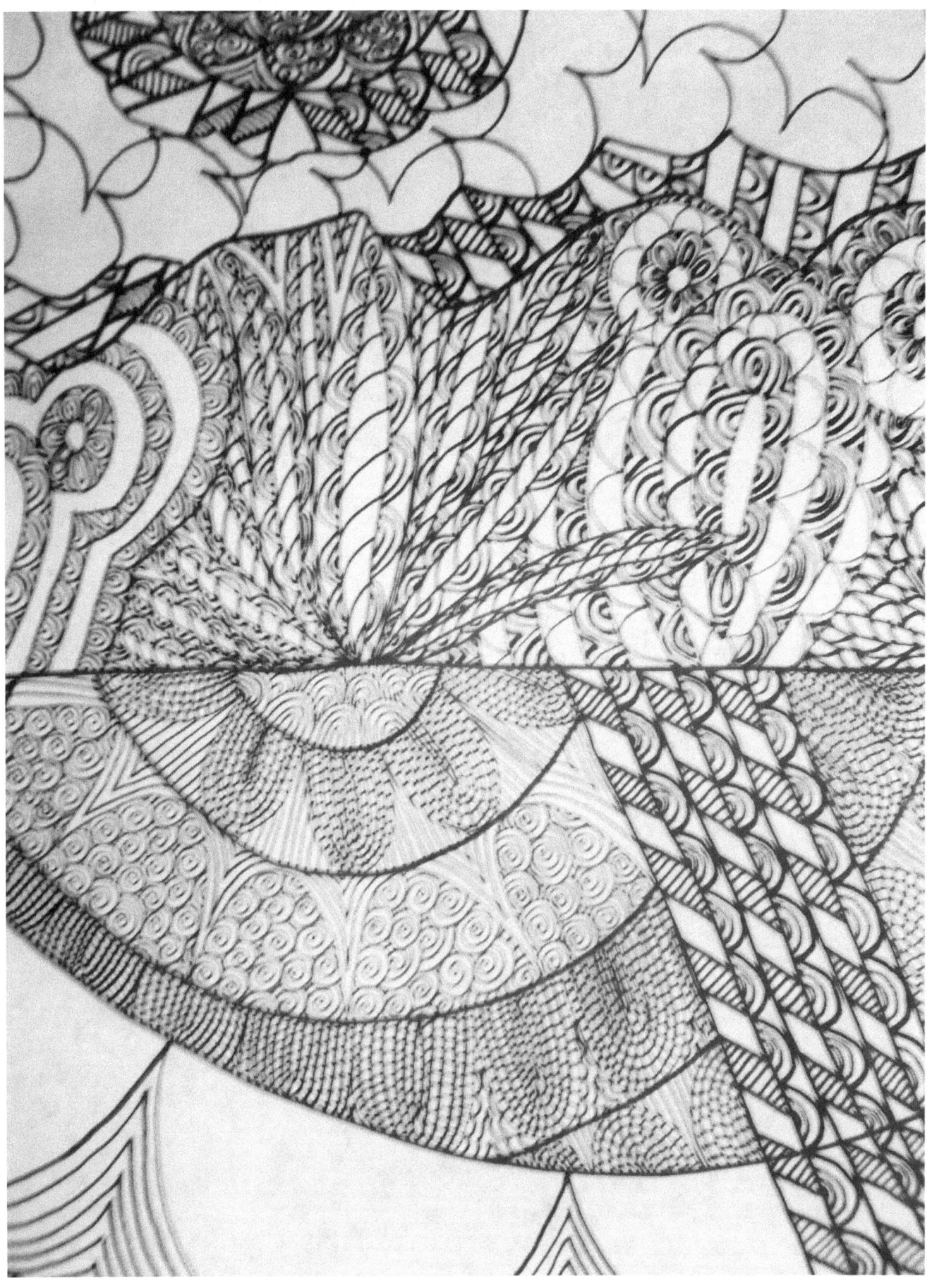

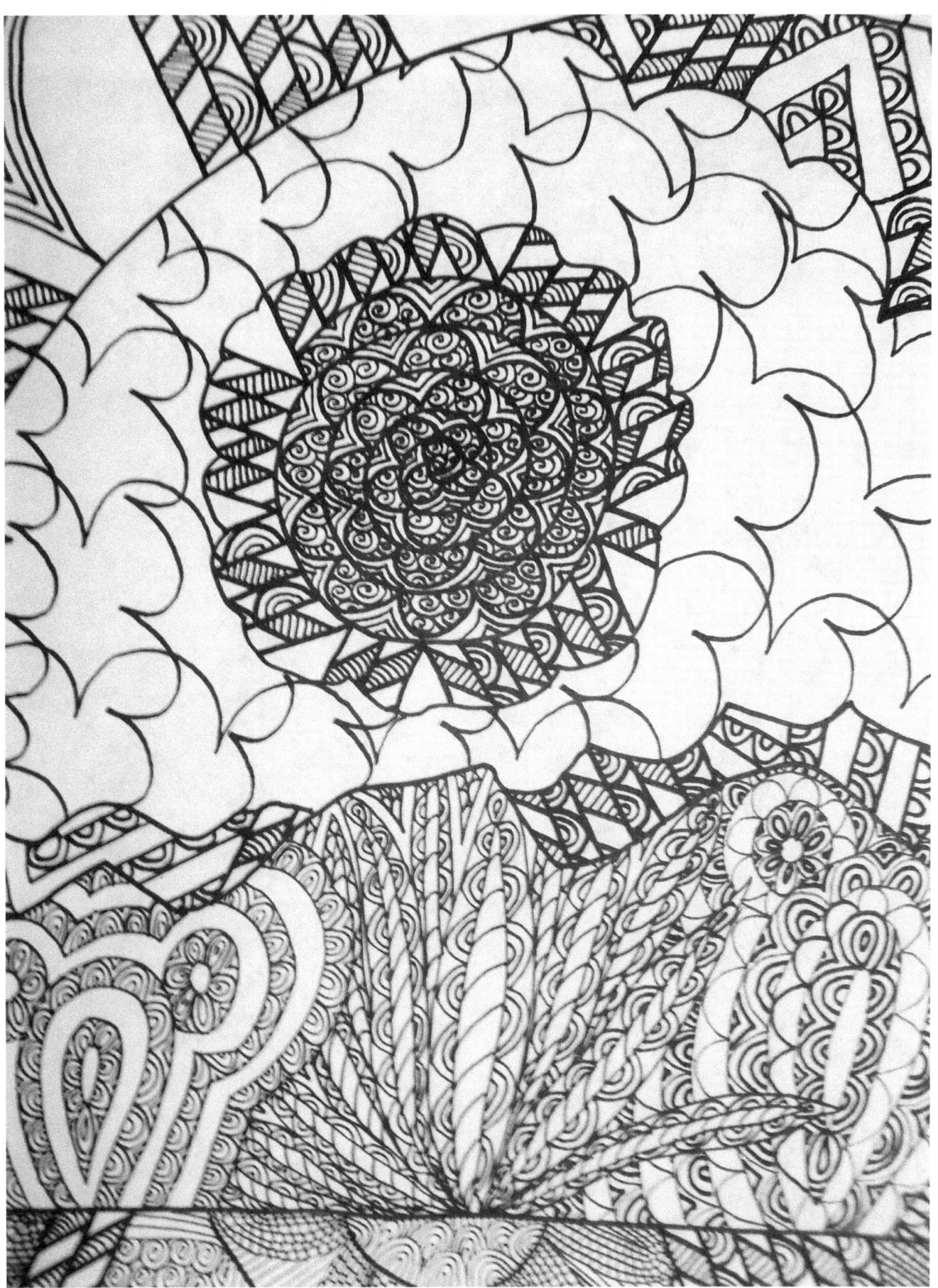

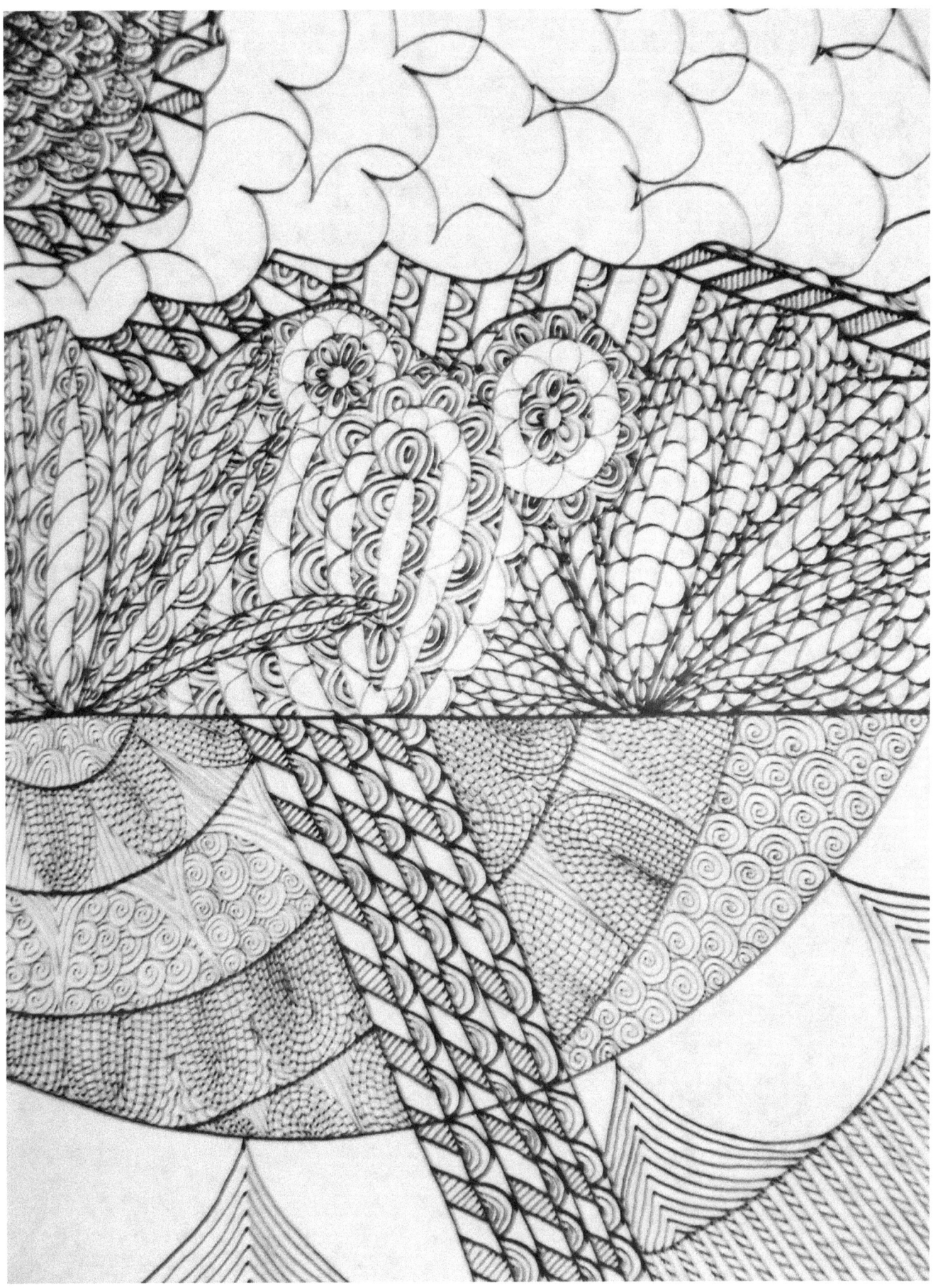

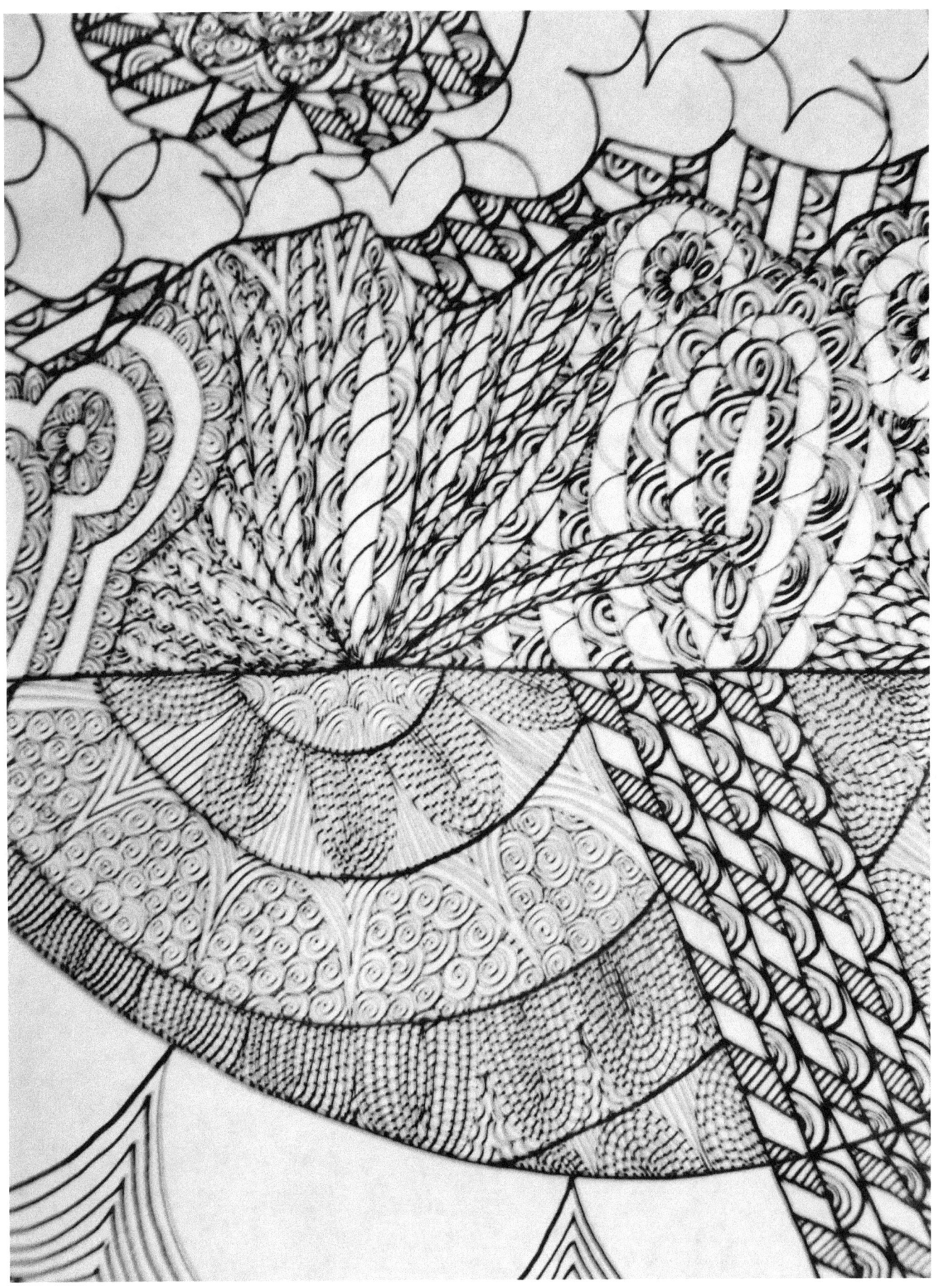

Bobby J. Jones

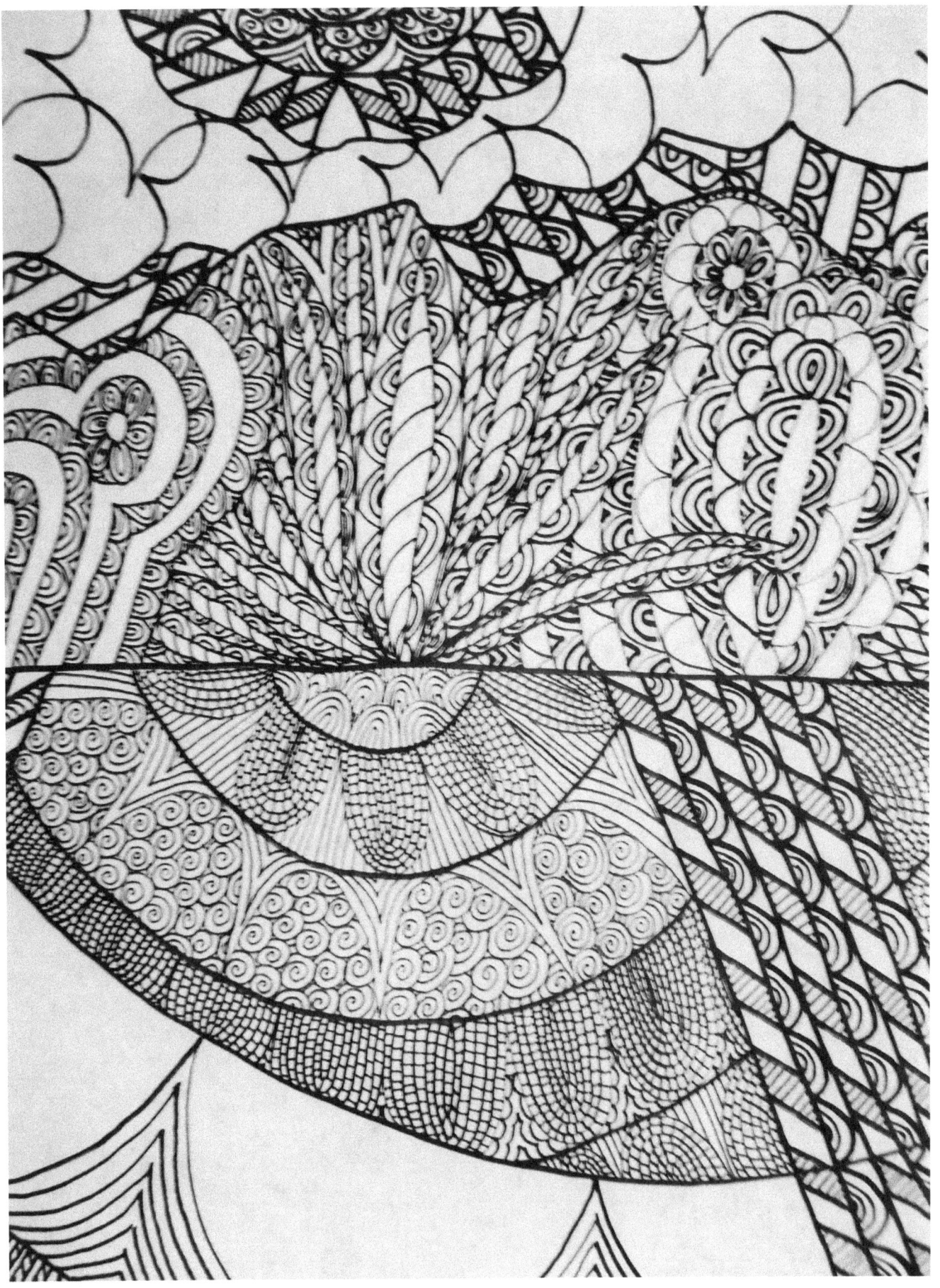

Bobby J. Jones

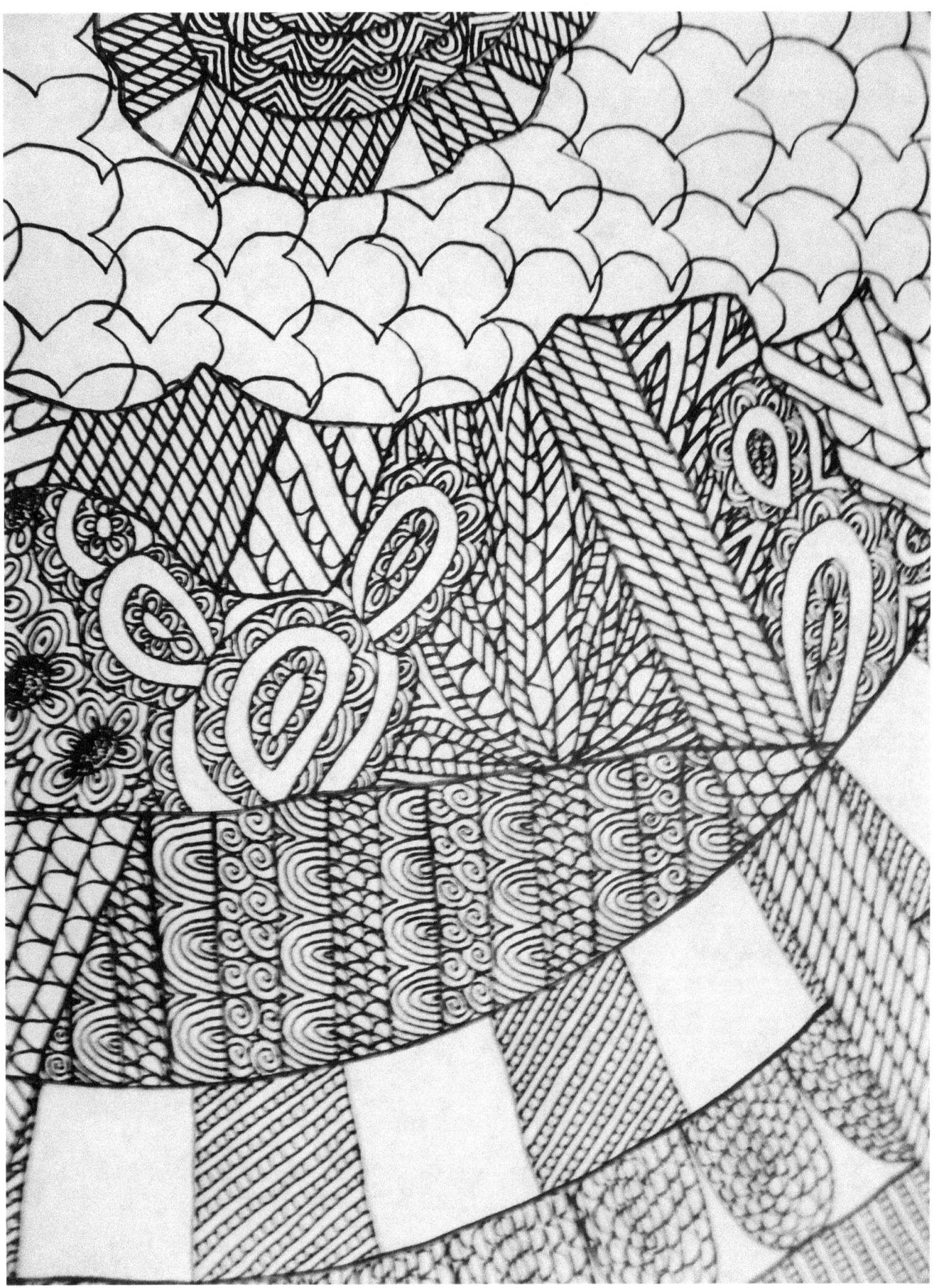

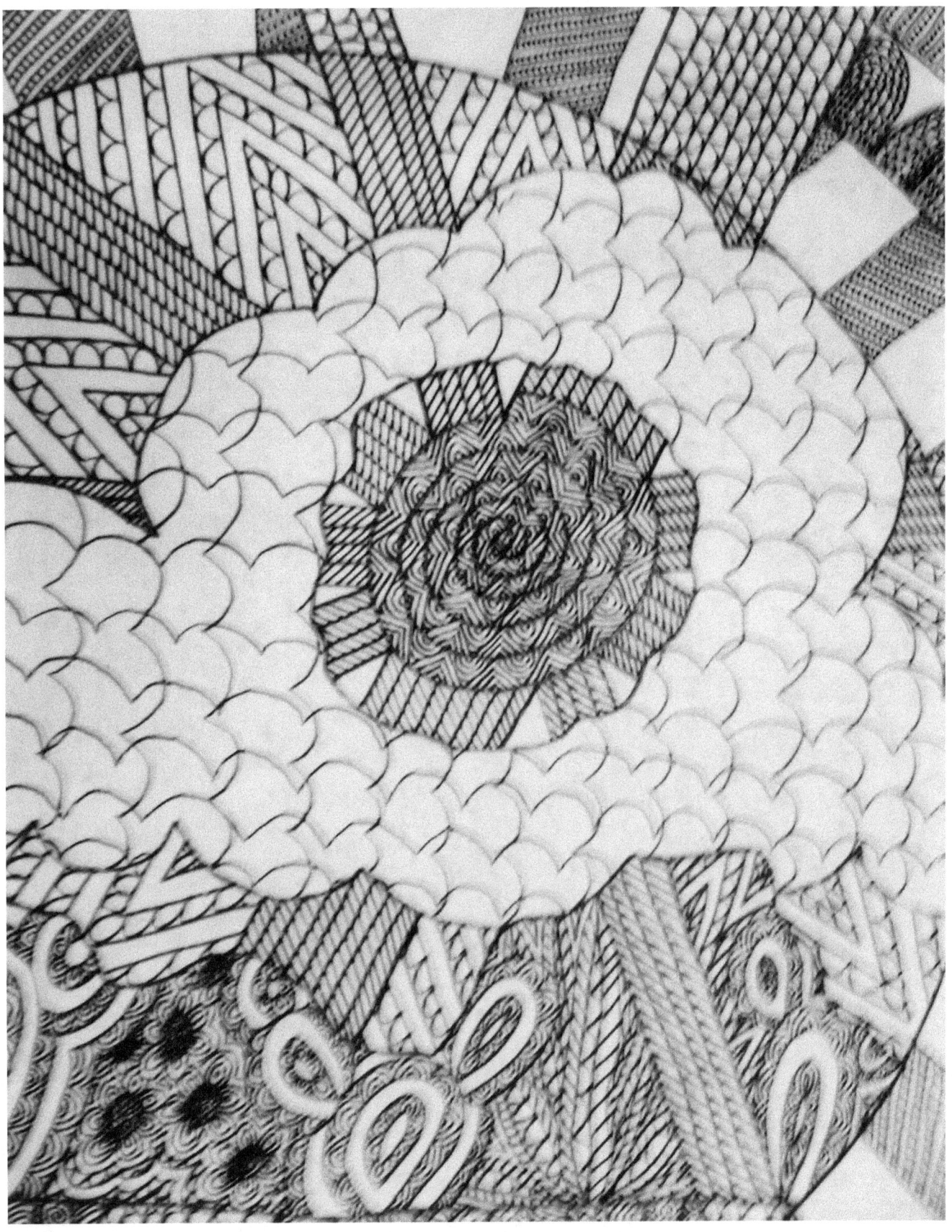

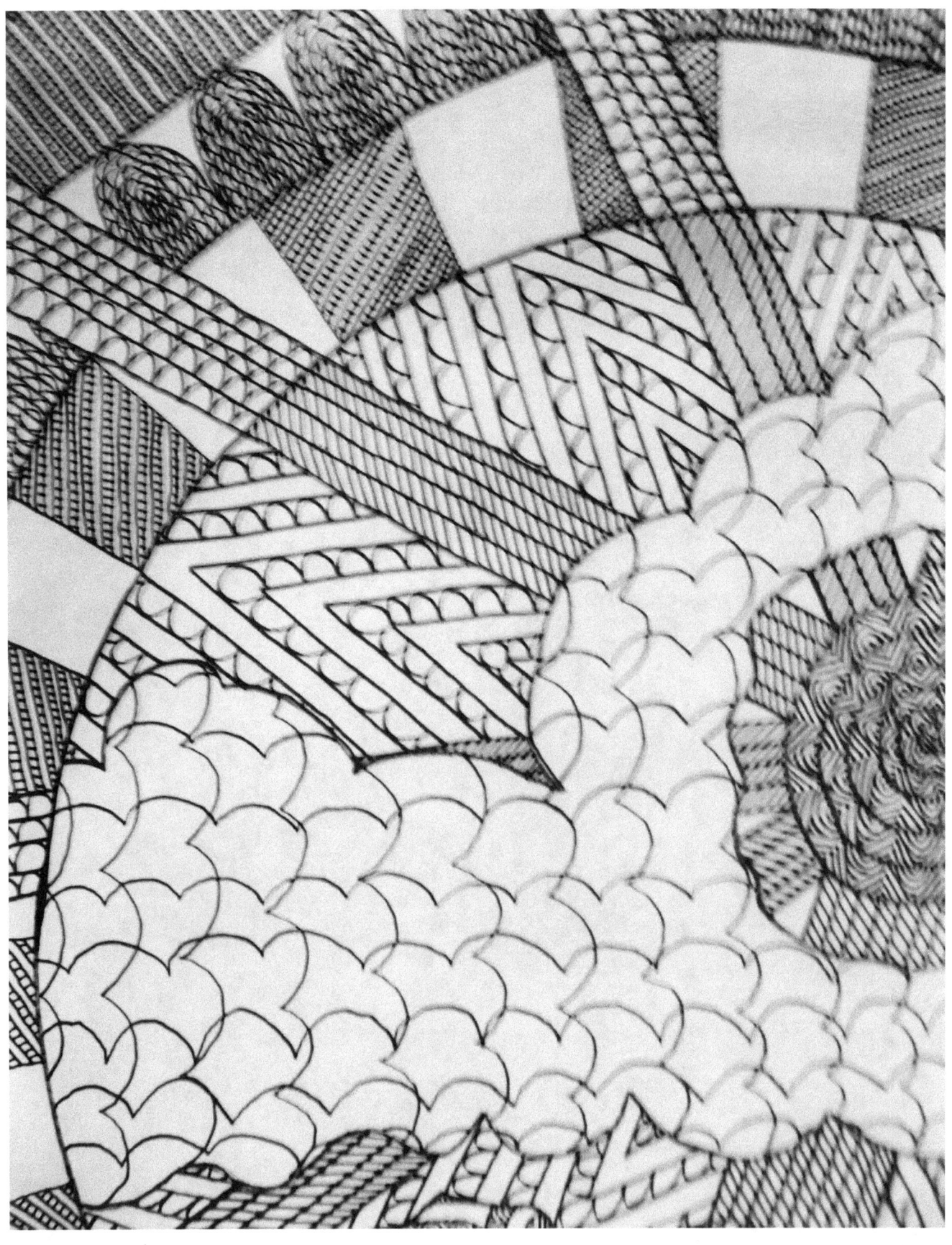

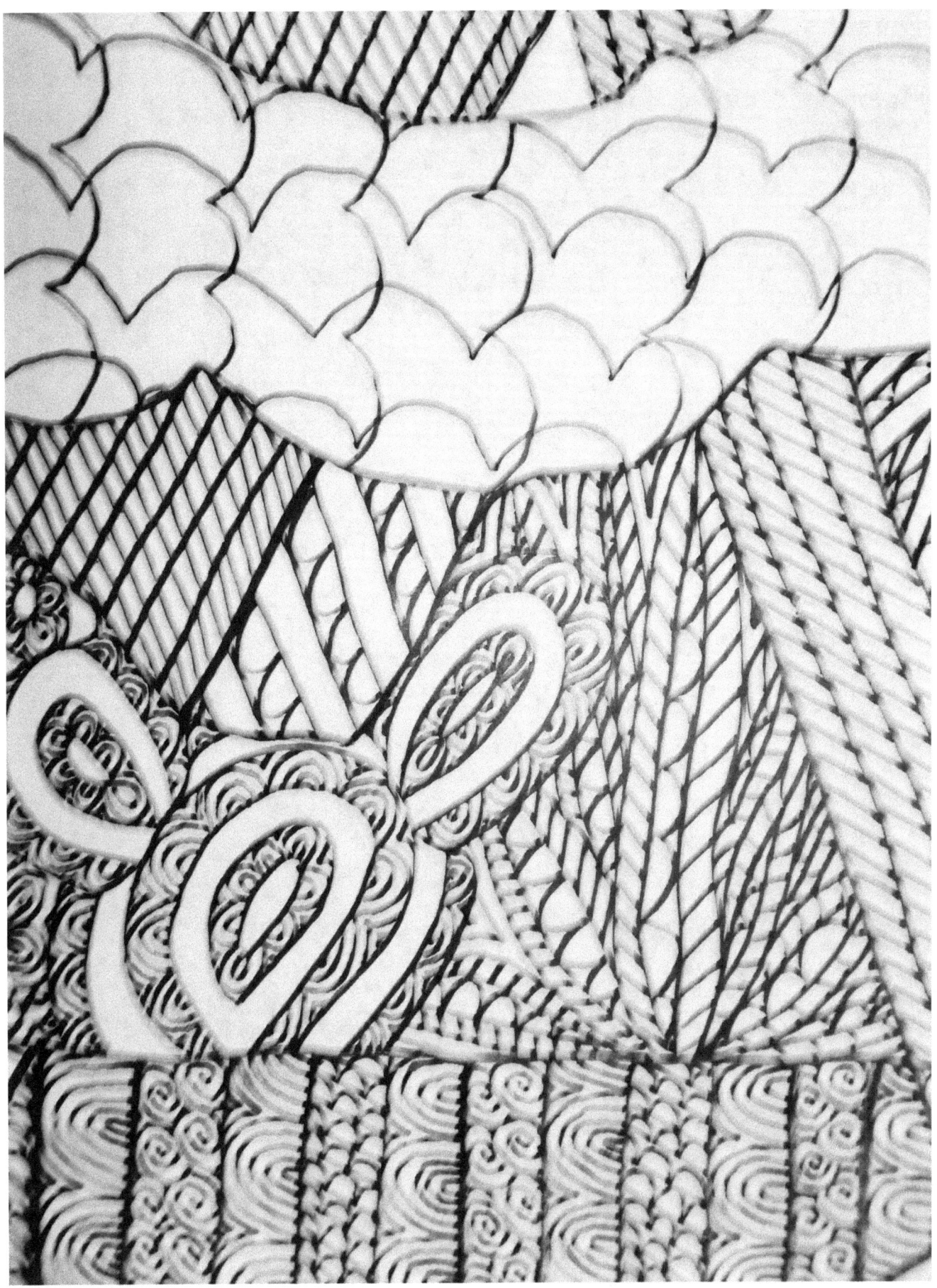

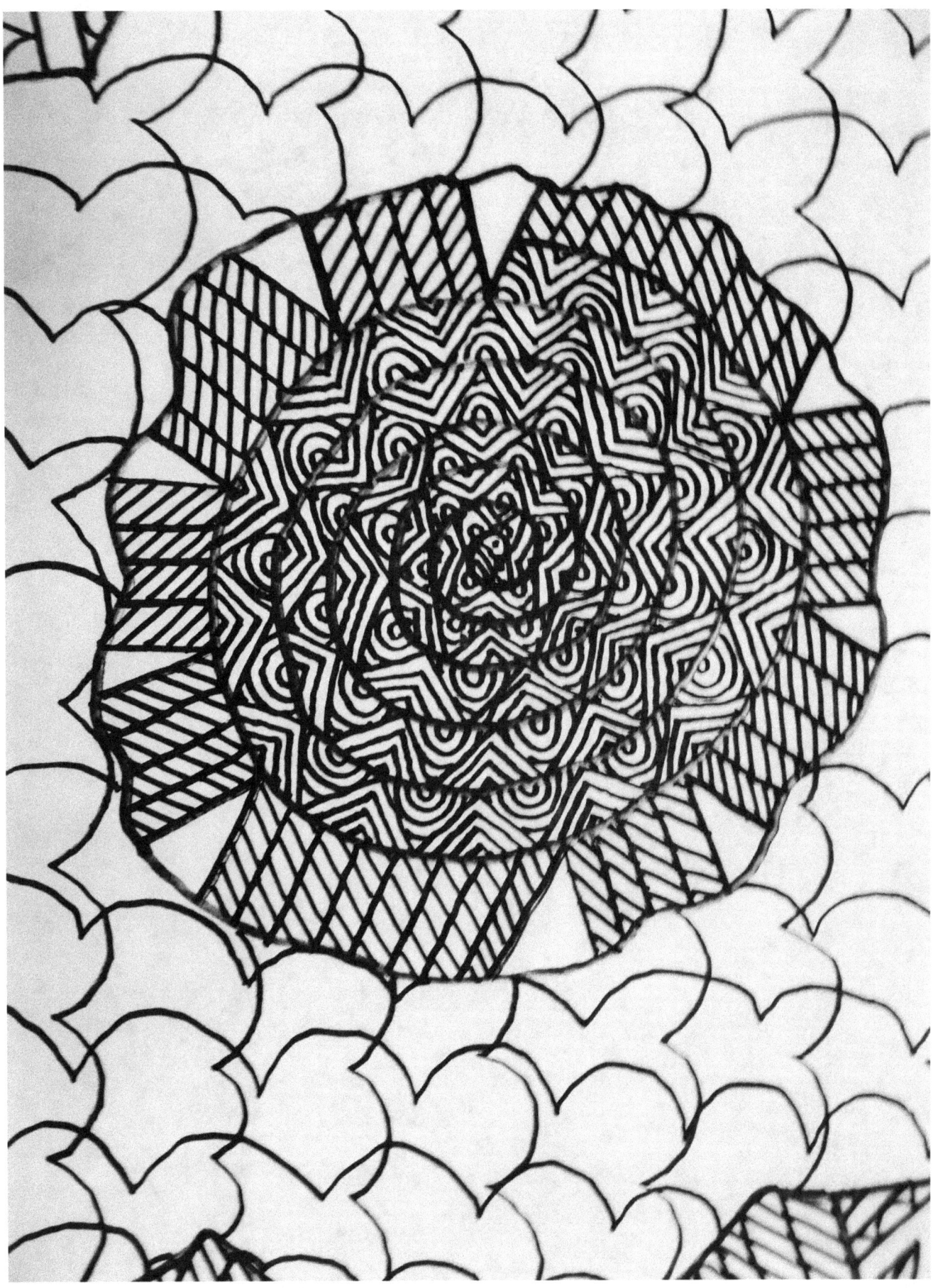

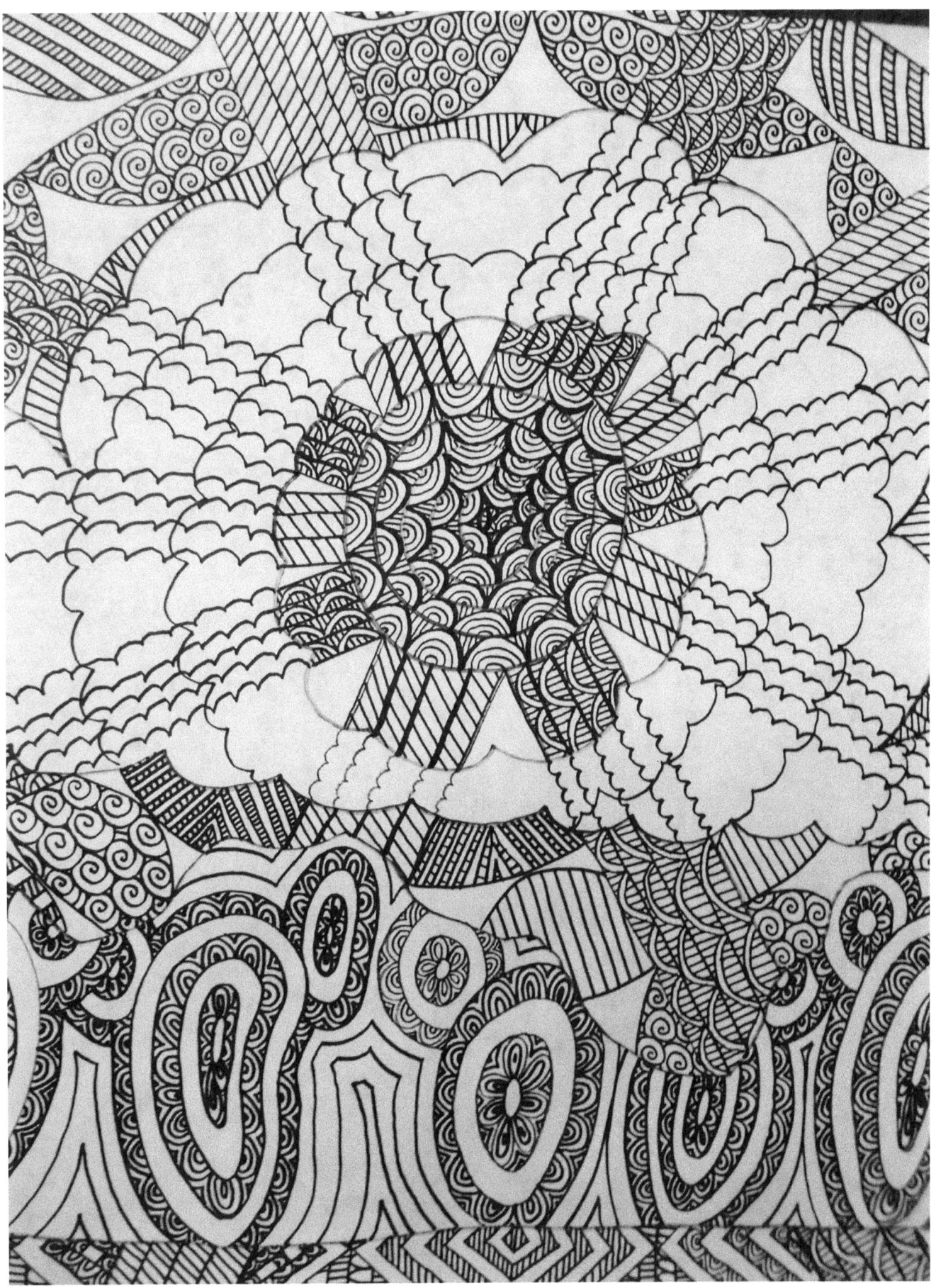

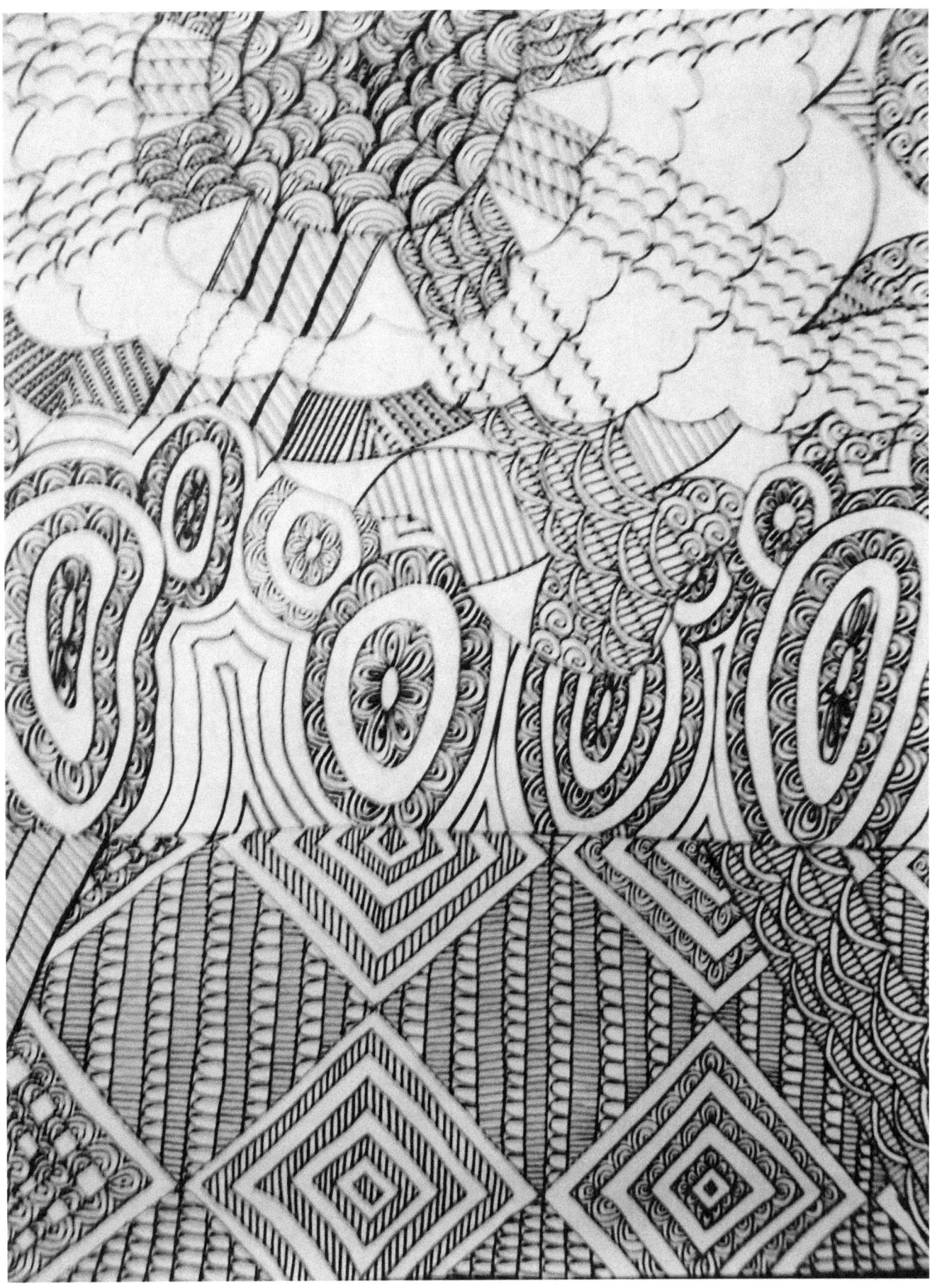

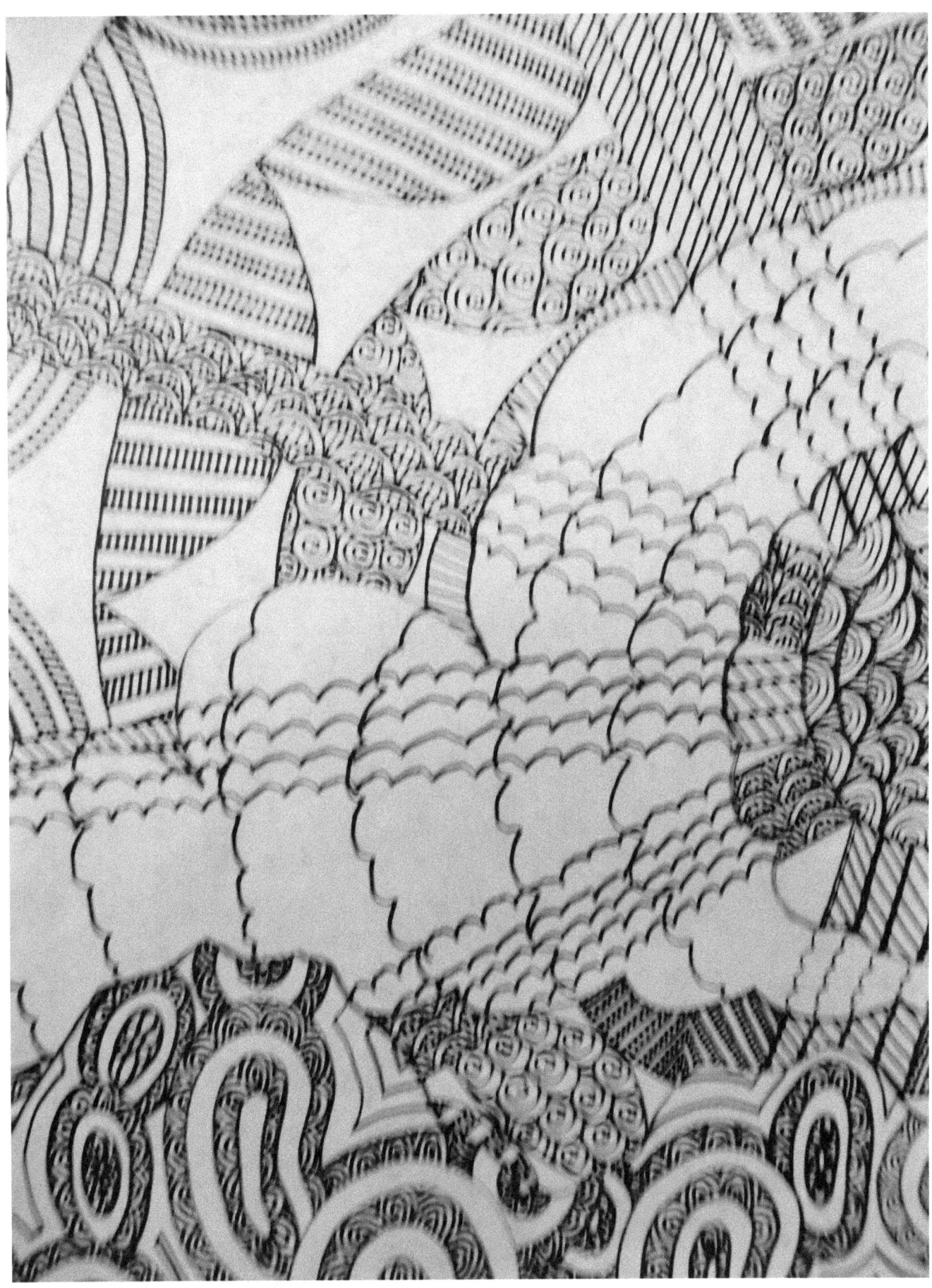

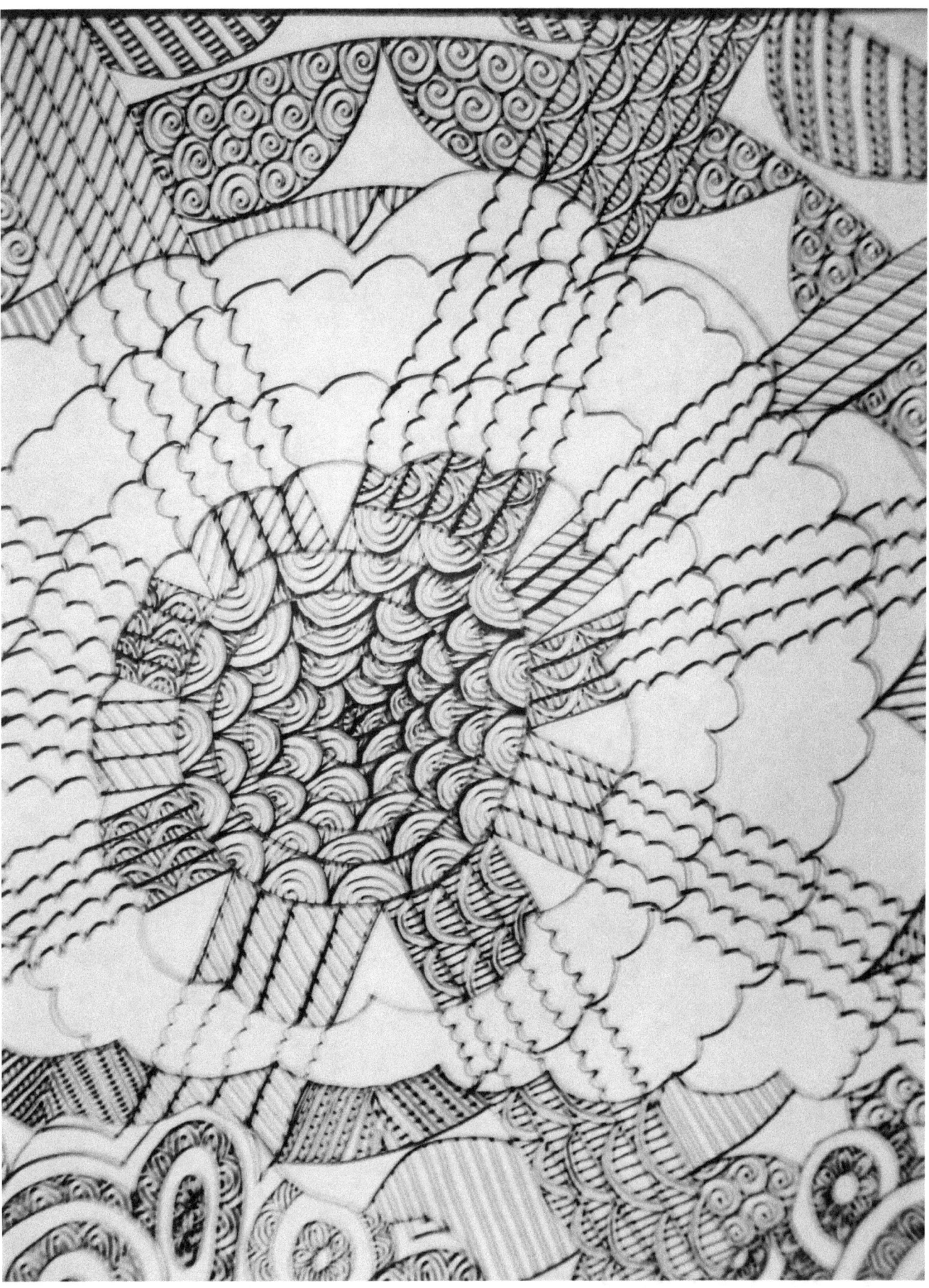

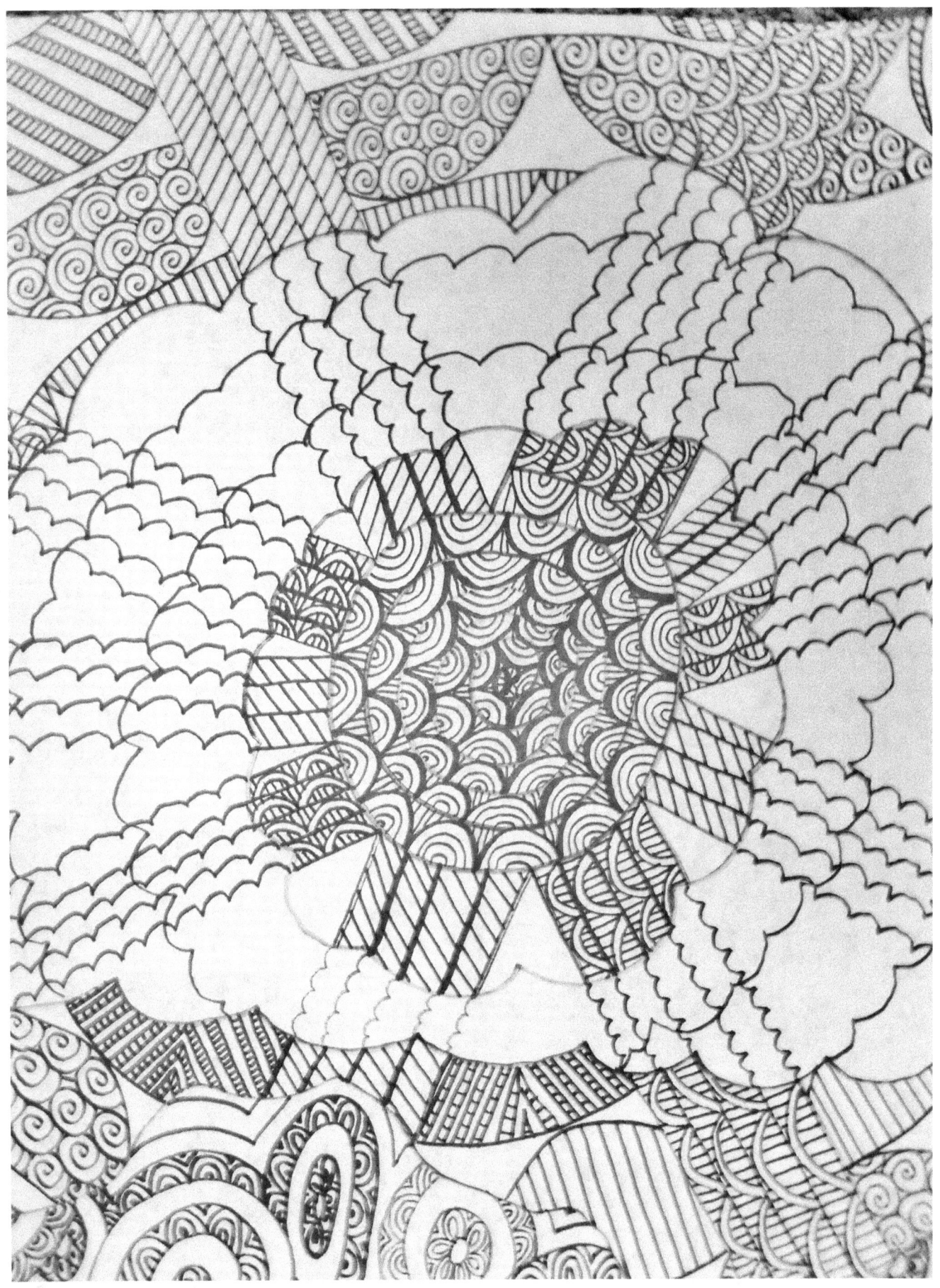

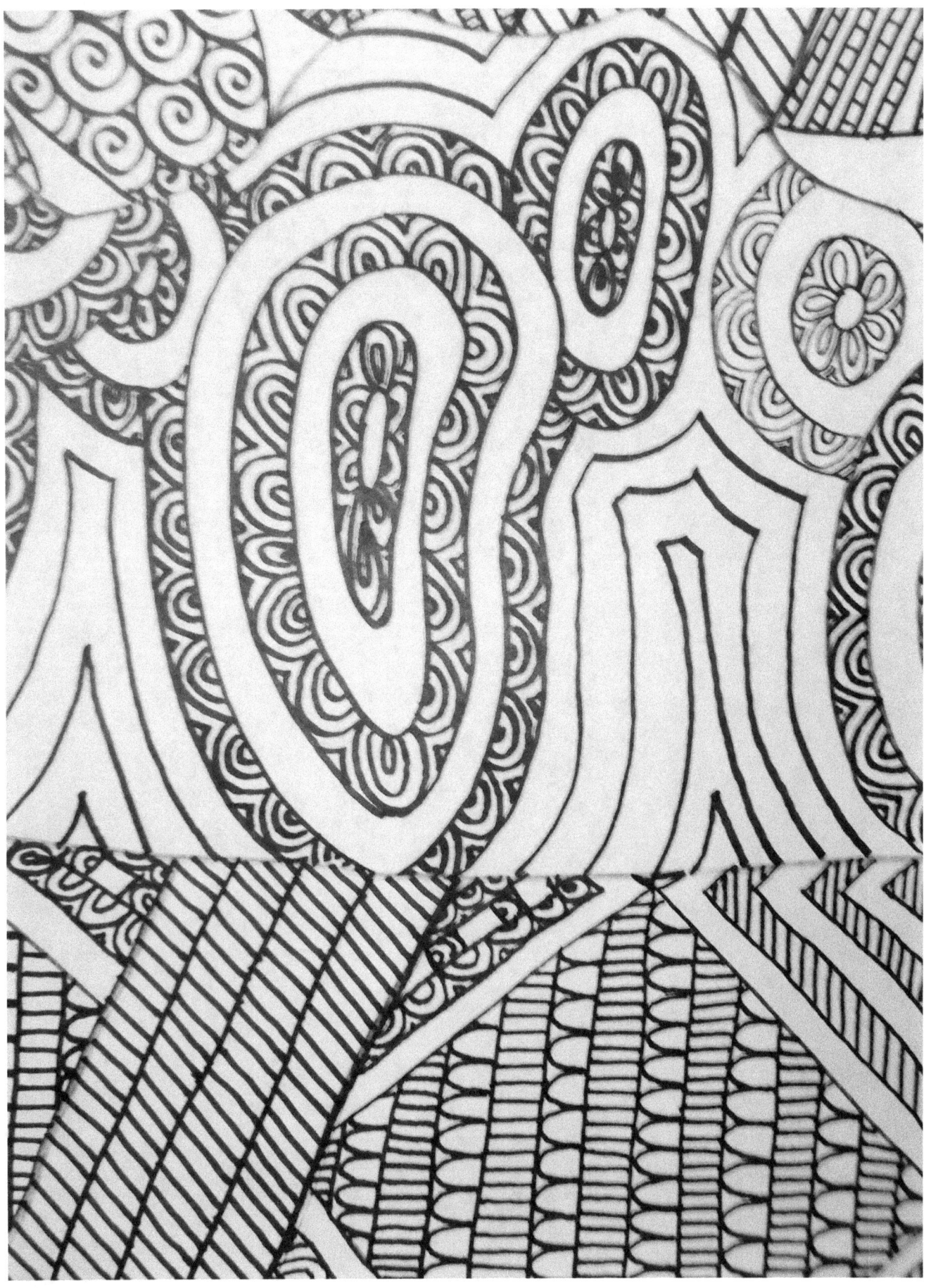

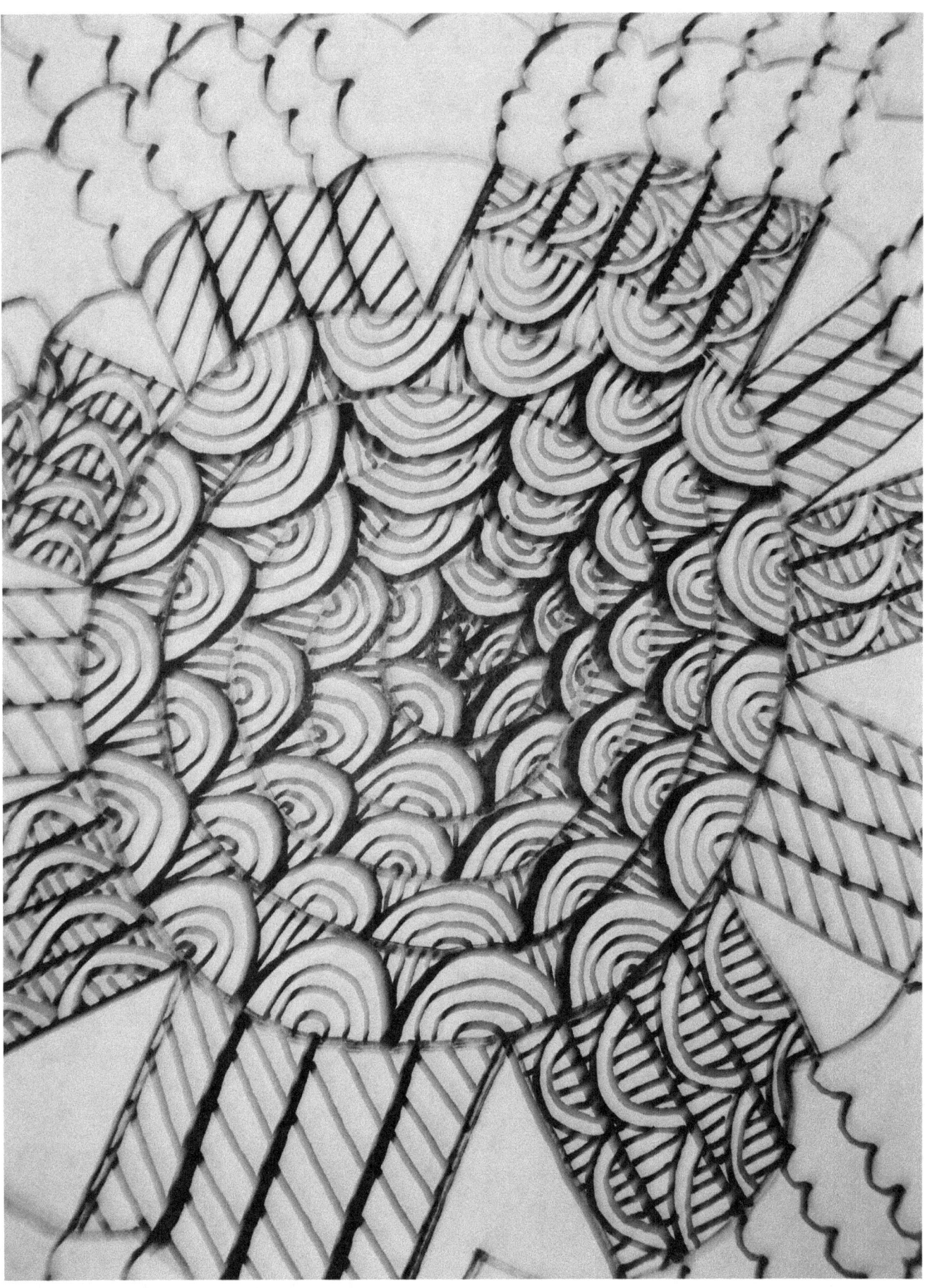

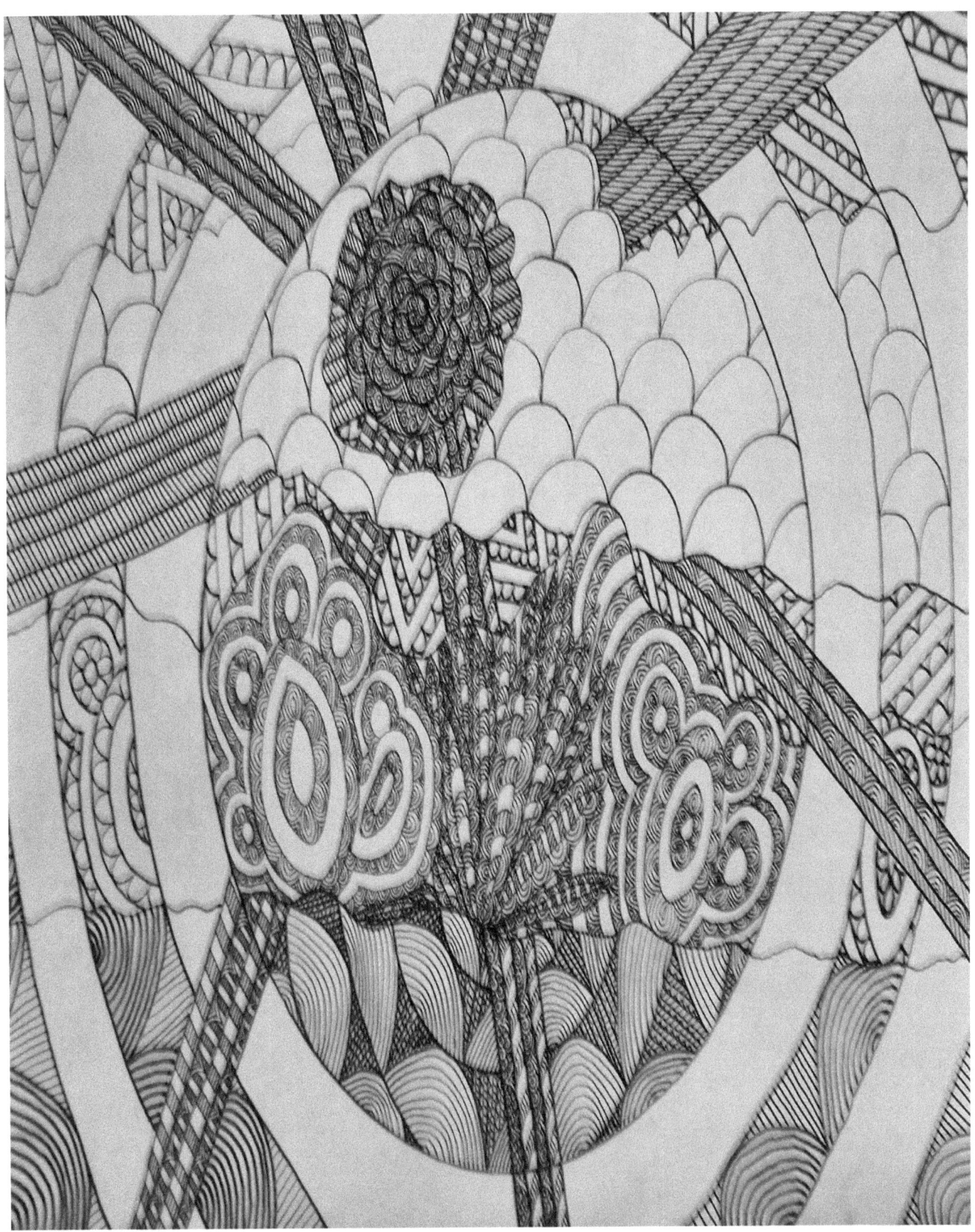

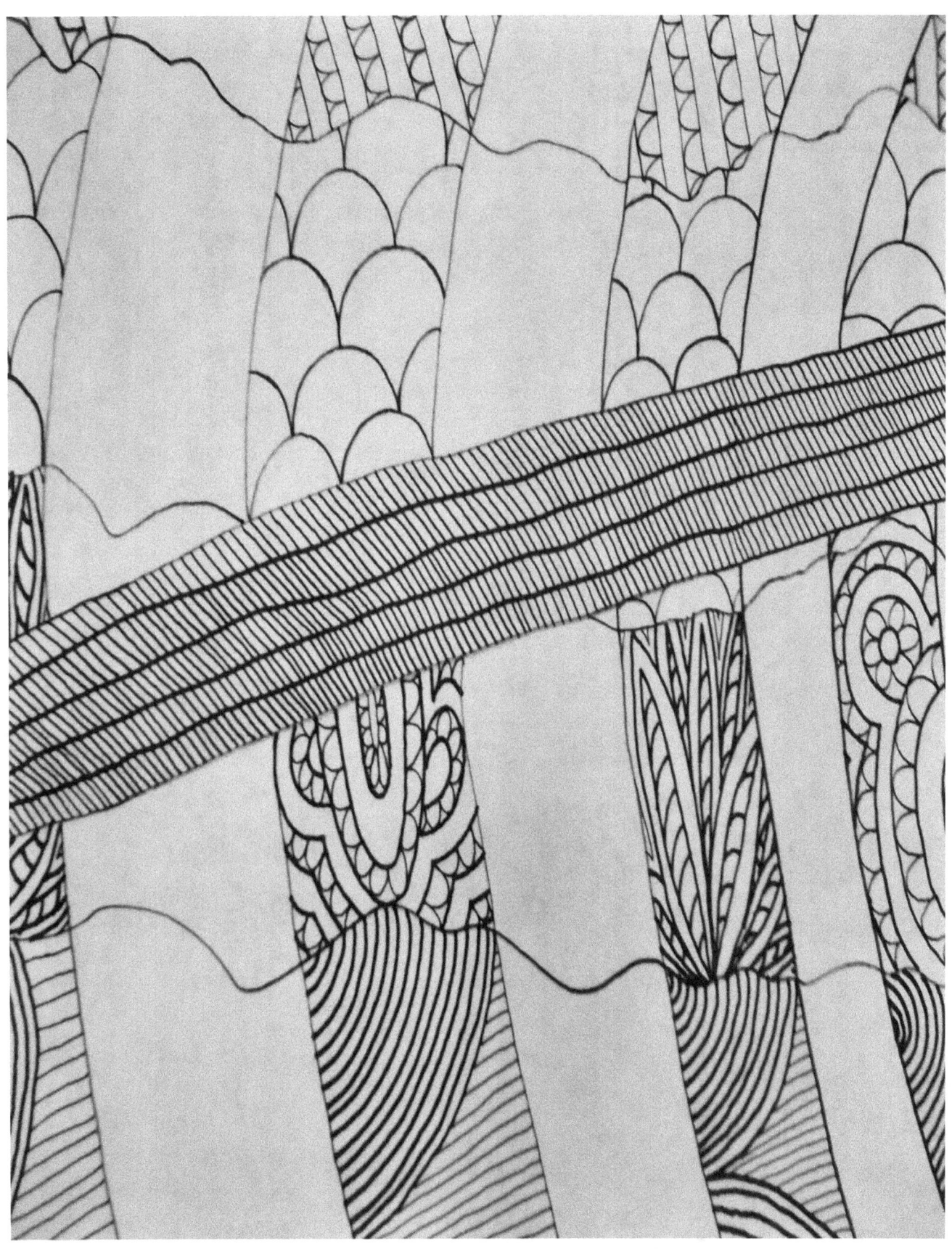

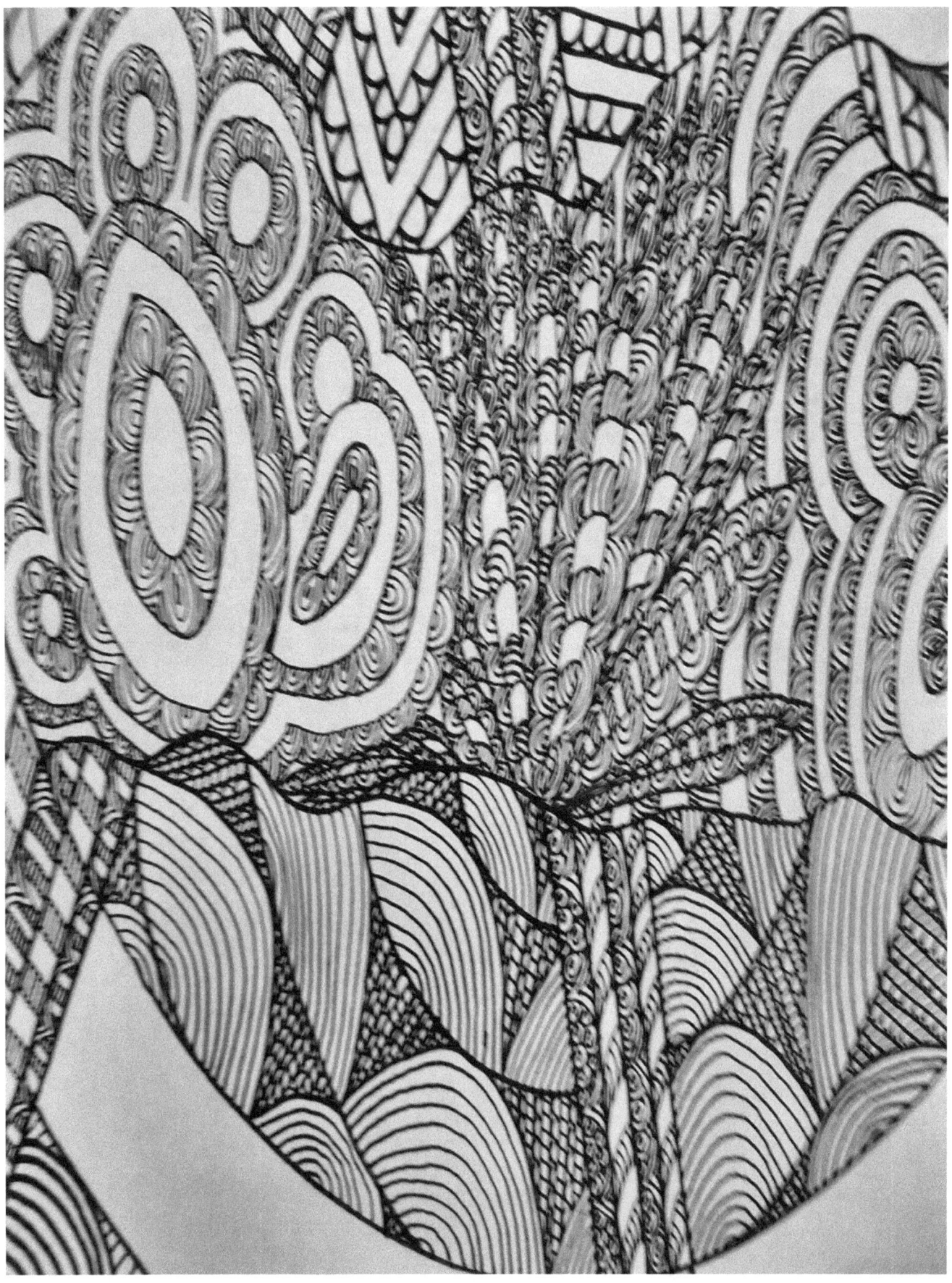

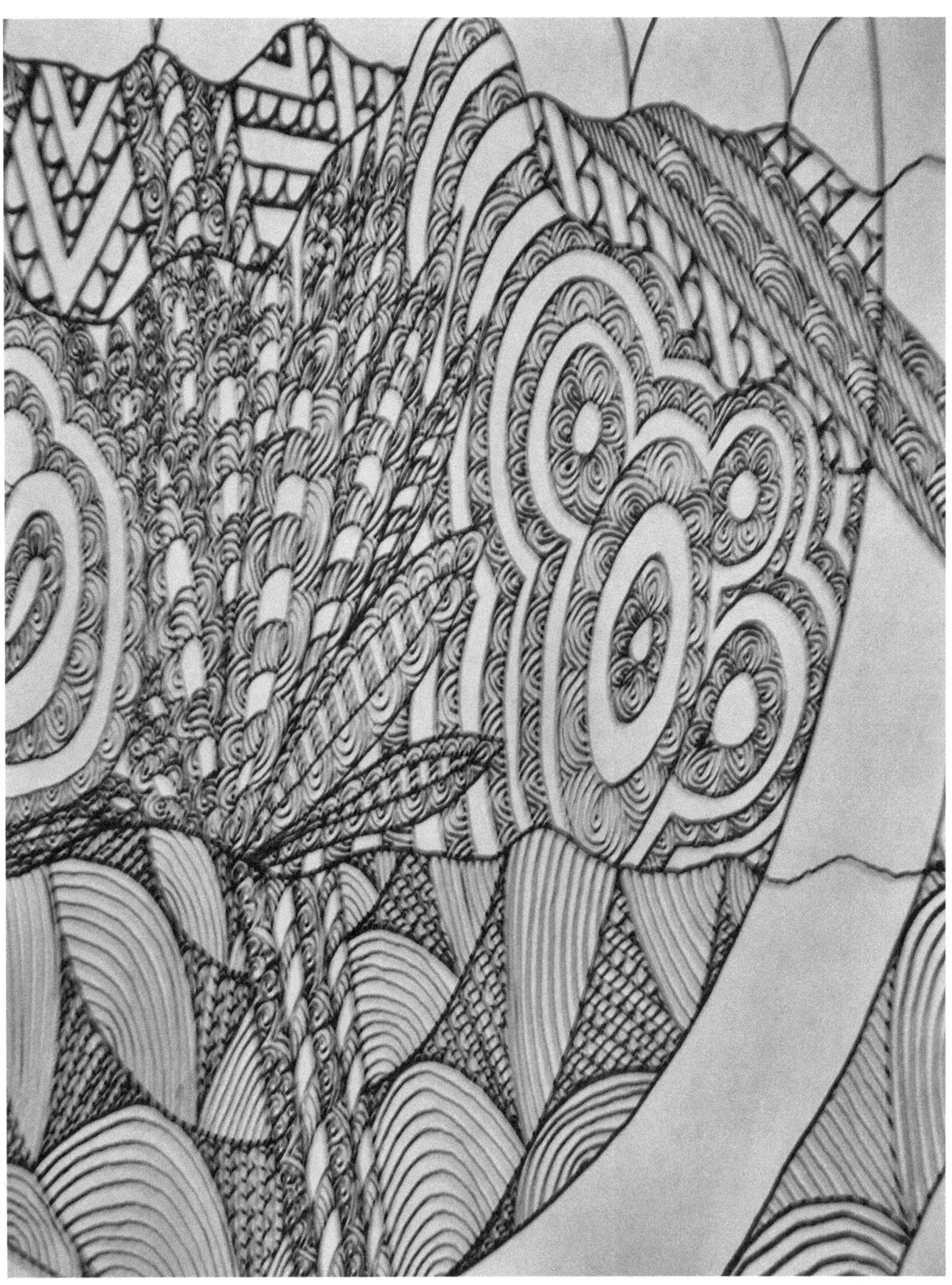

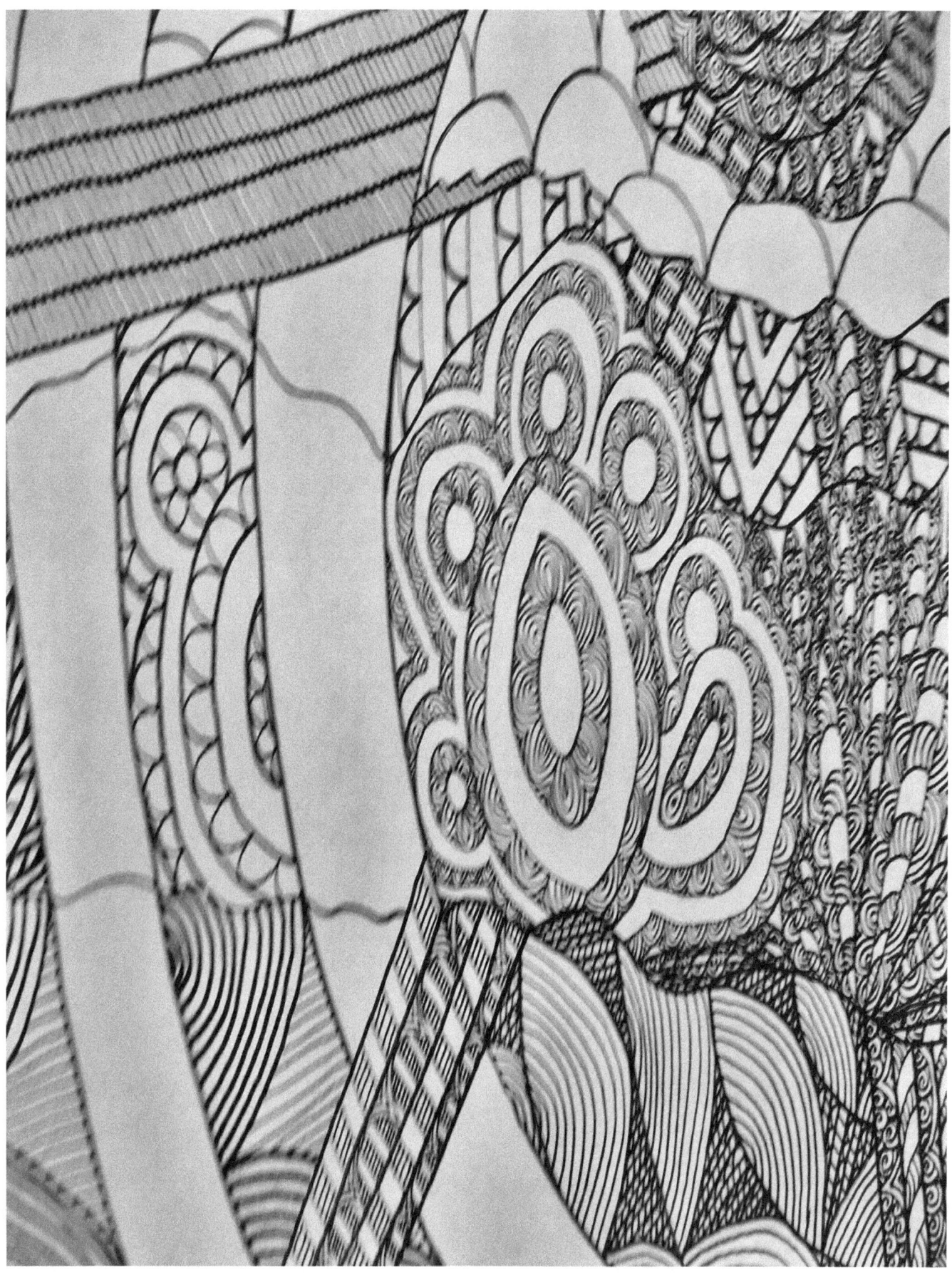

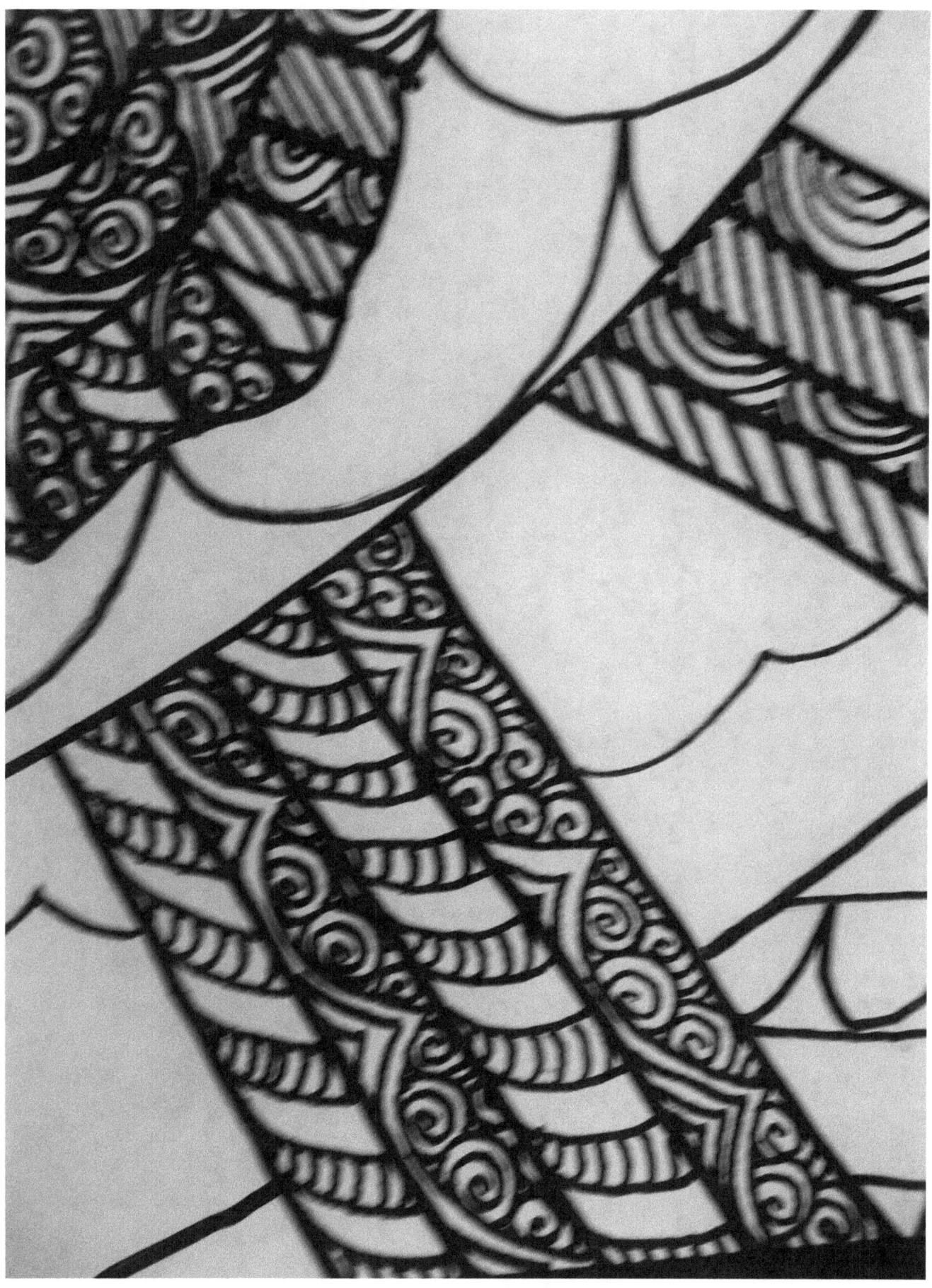

Bobby J. Jones

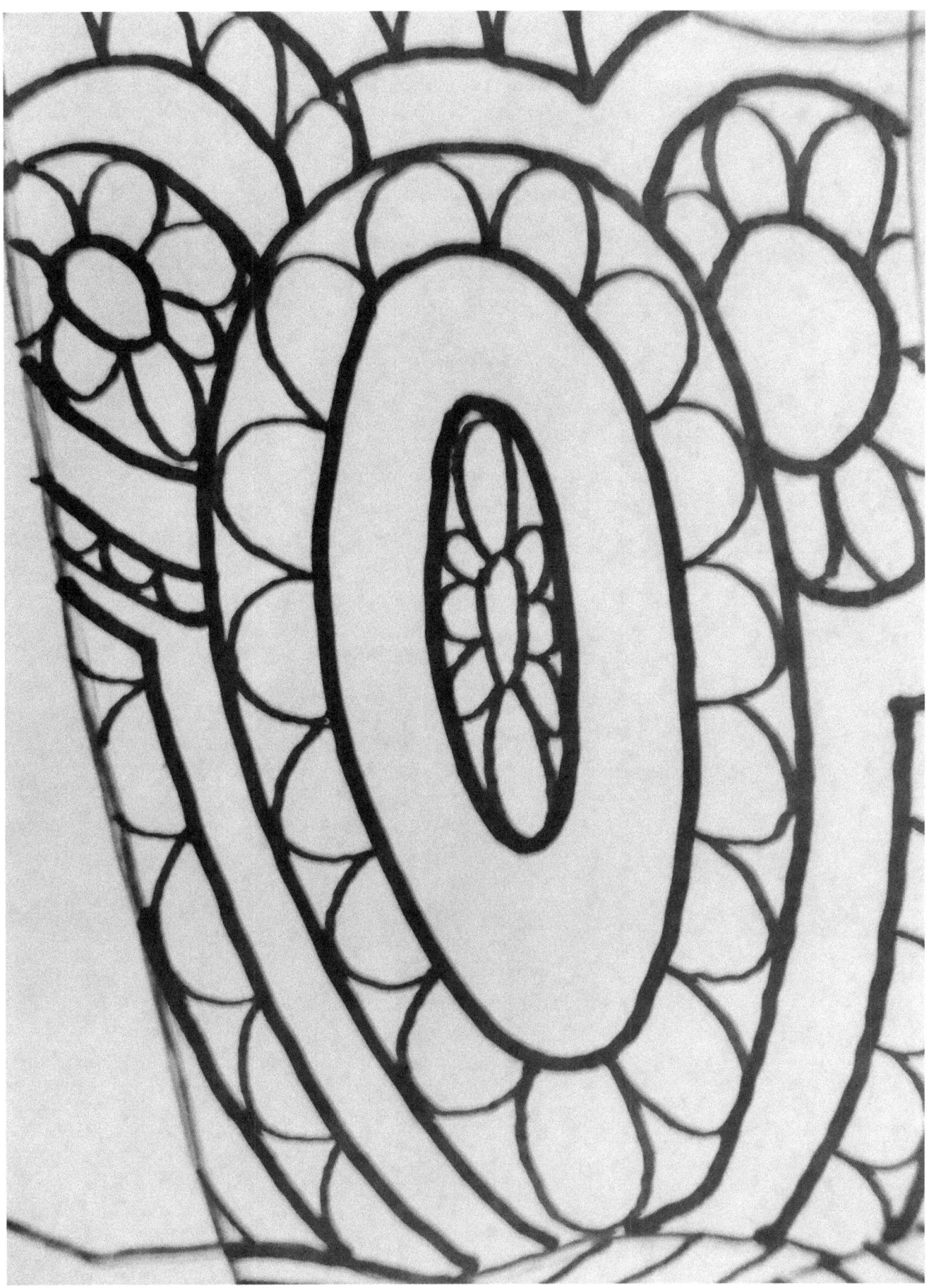

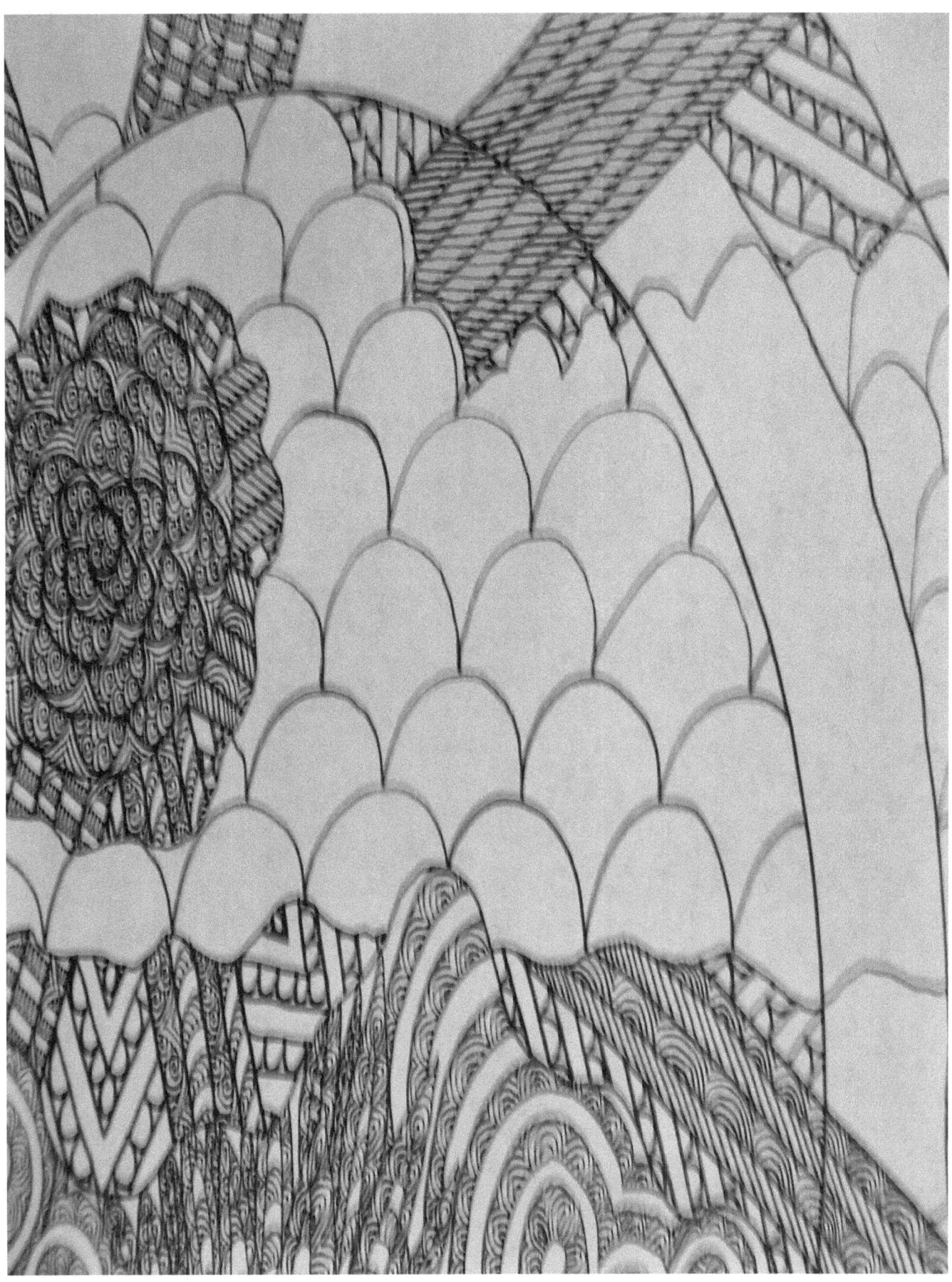

Bobby J. Jones

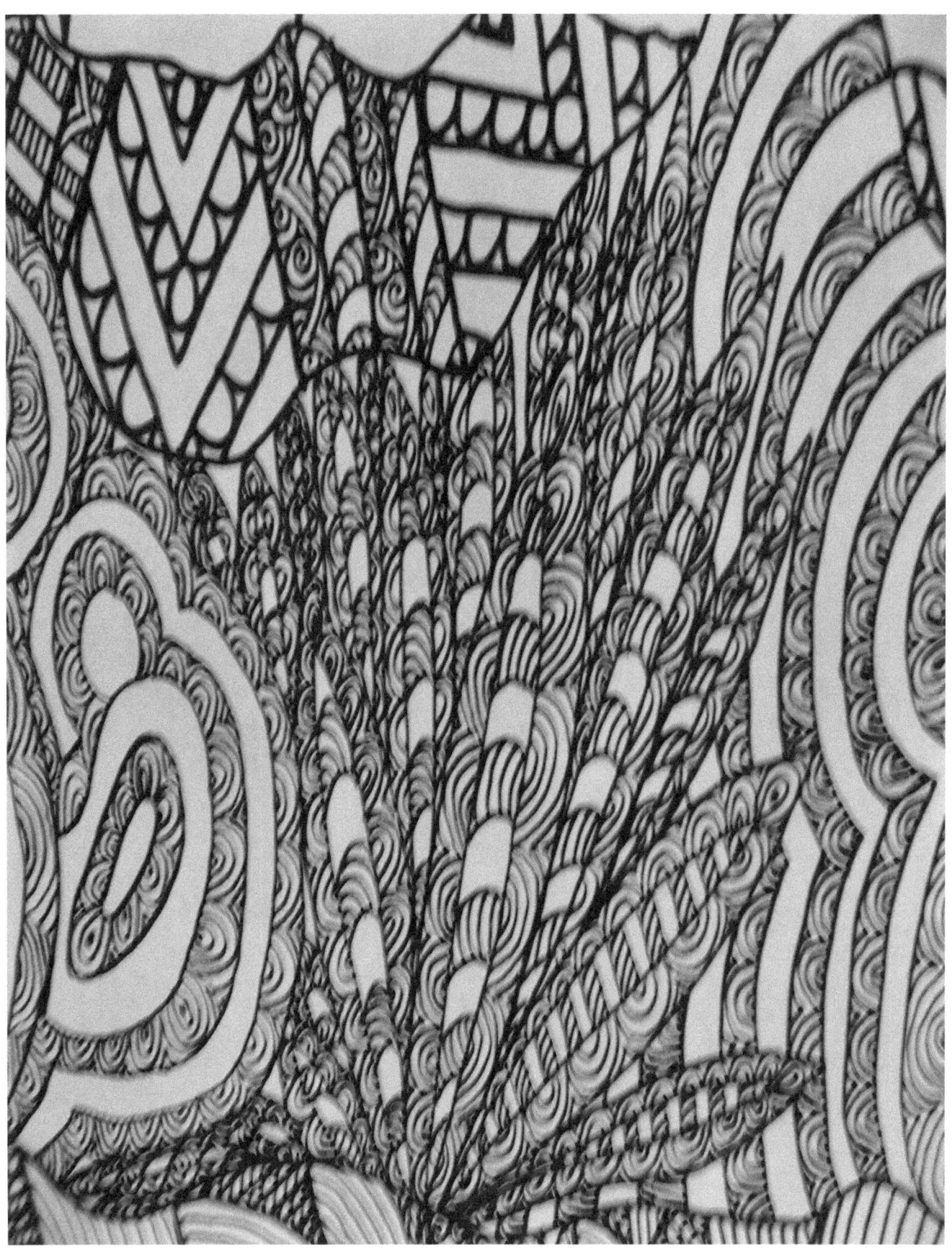

Bobby J. Jones

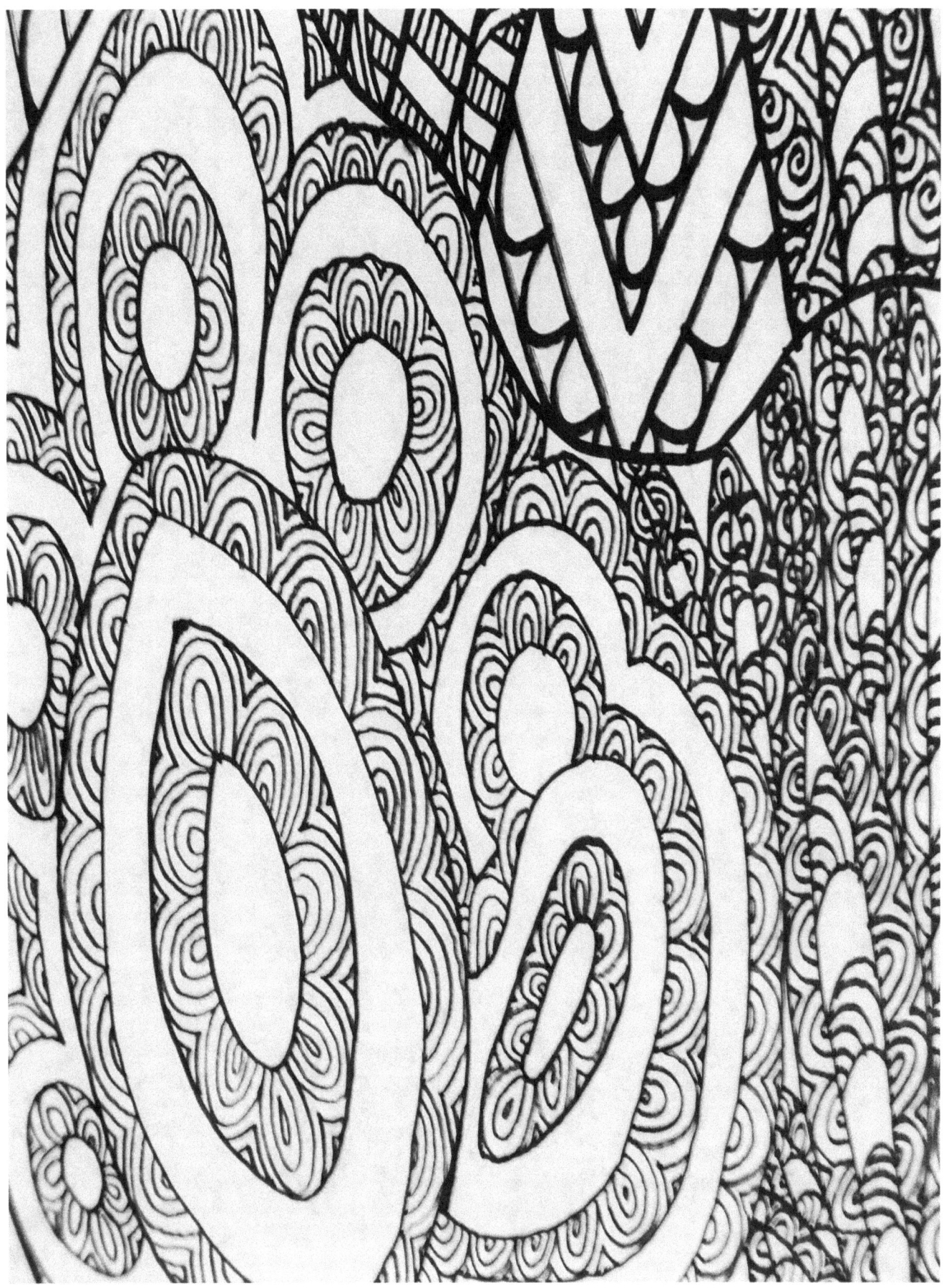

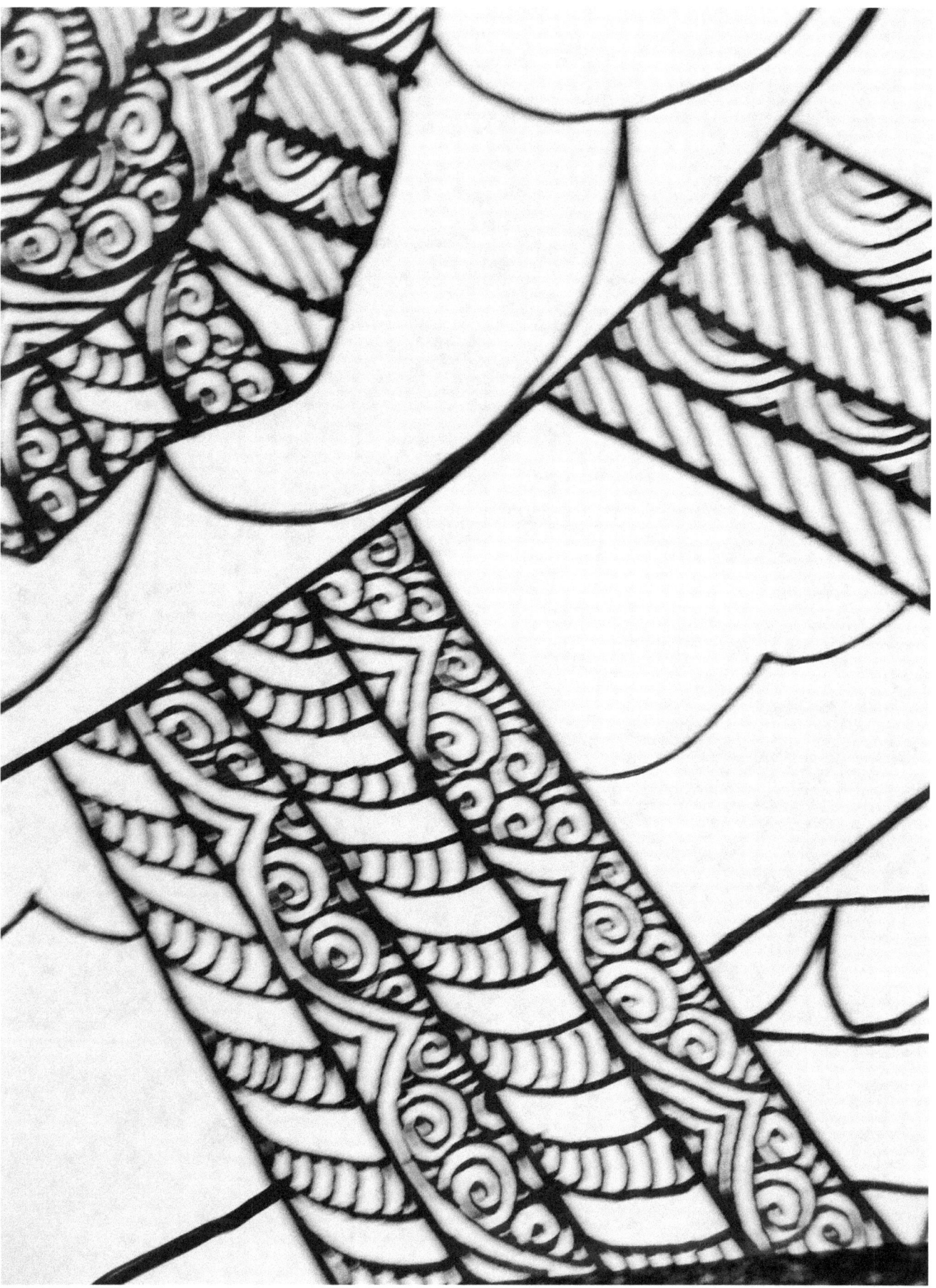

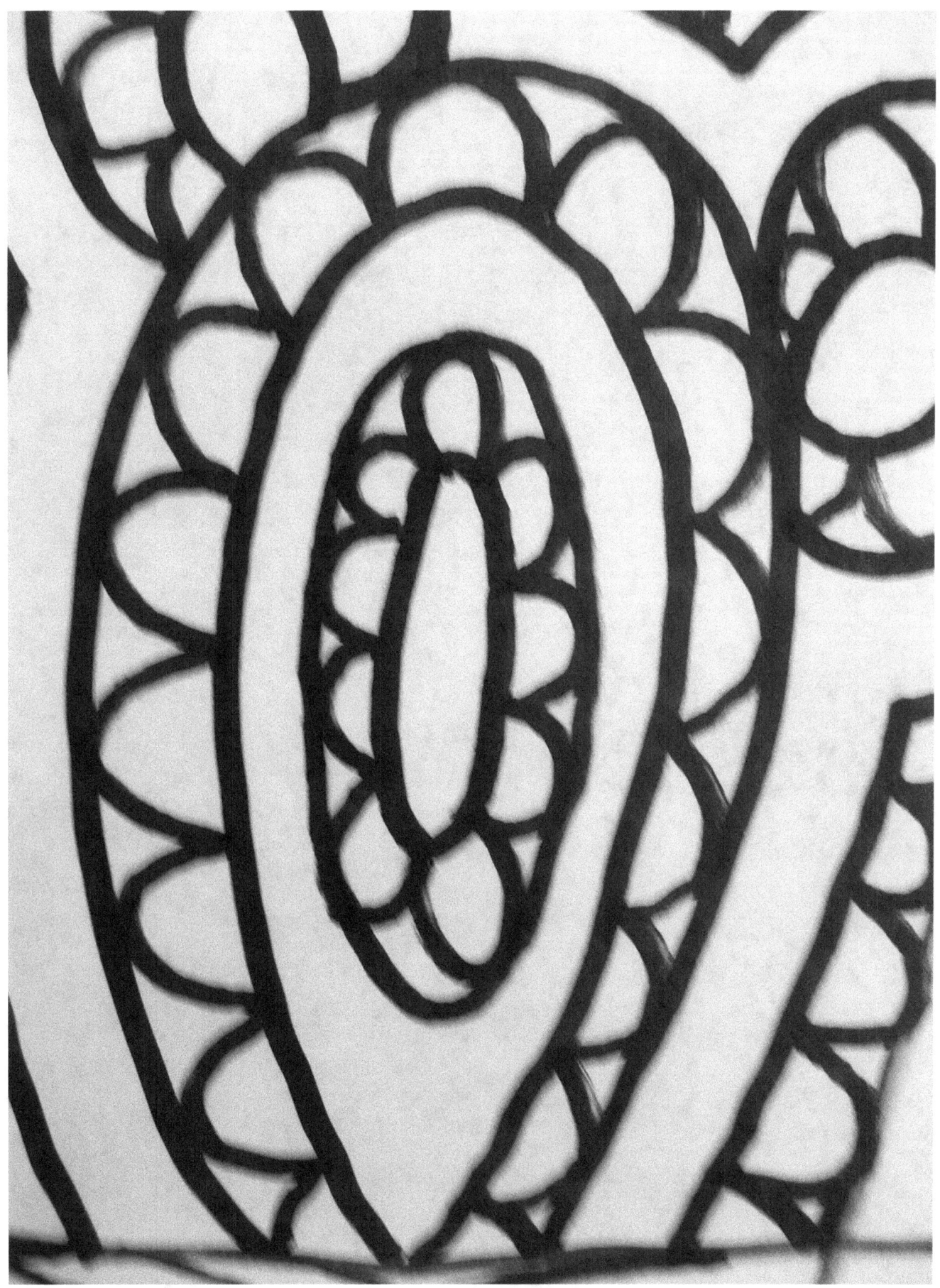

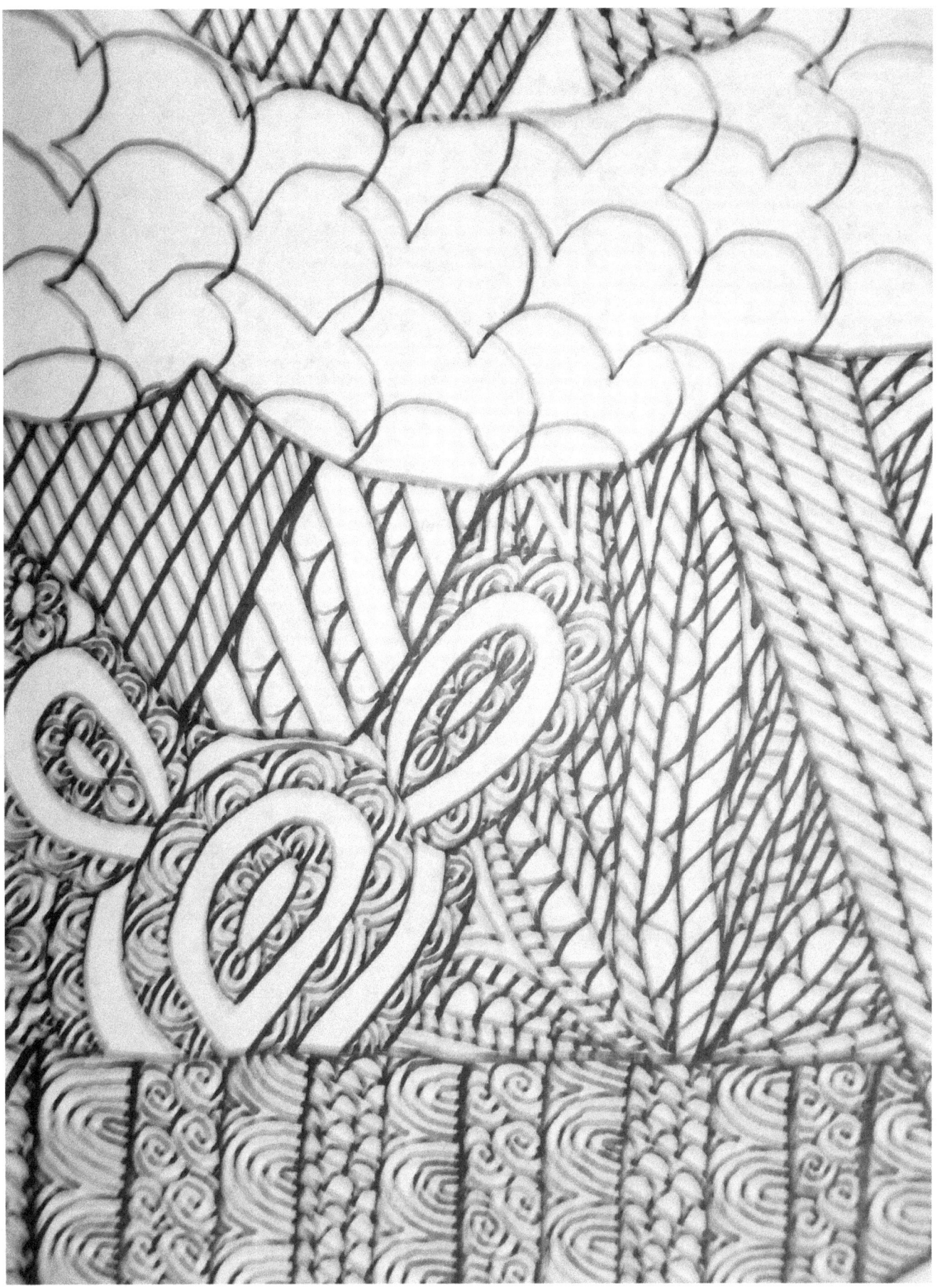

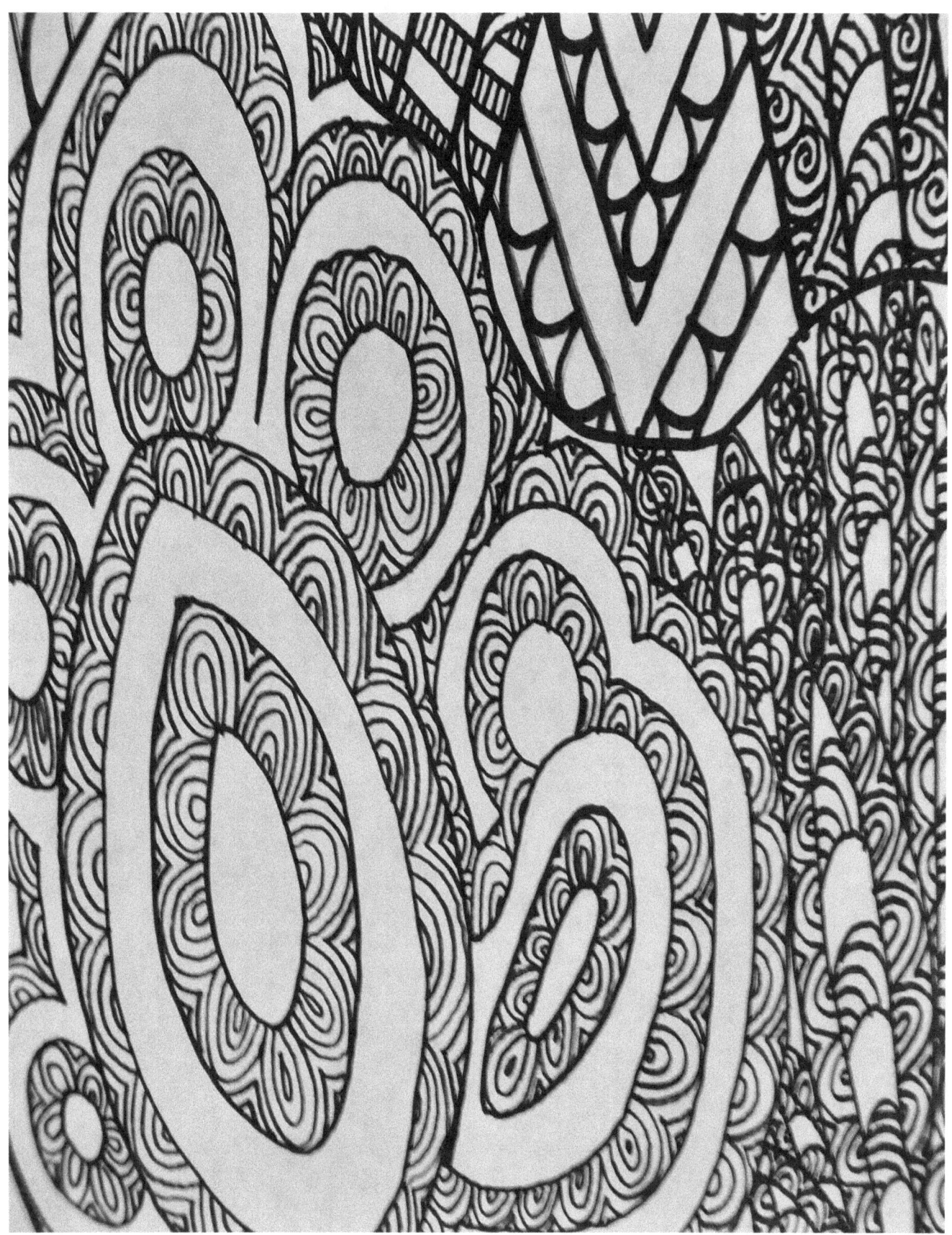

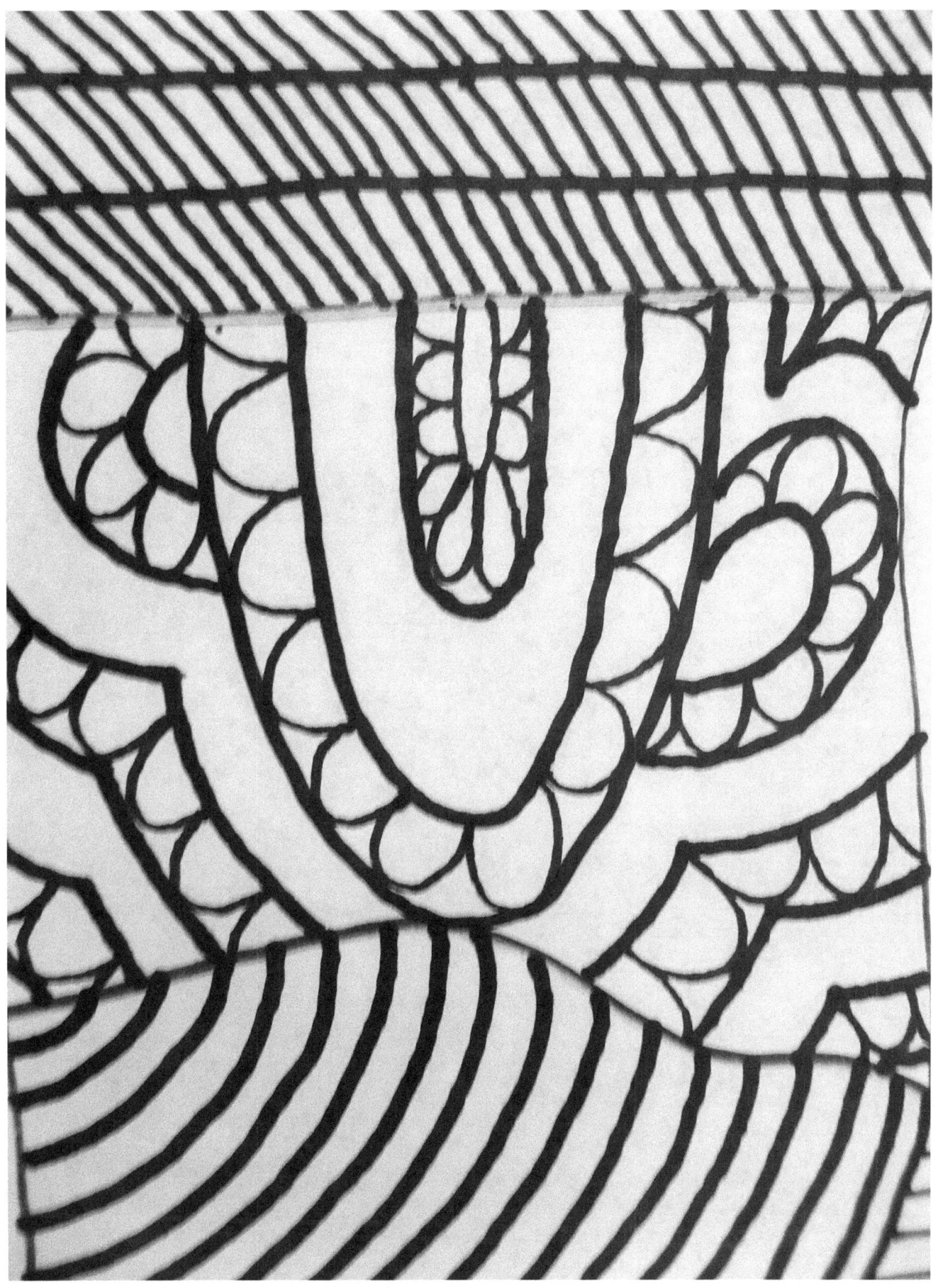

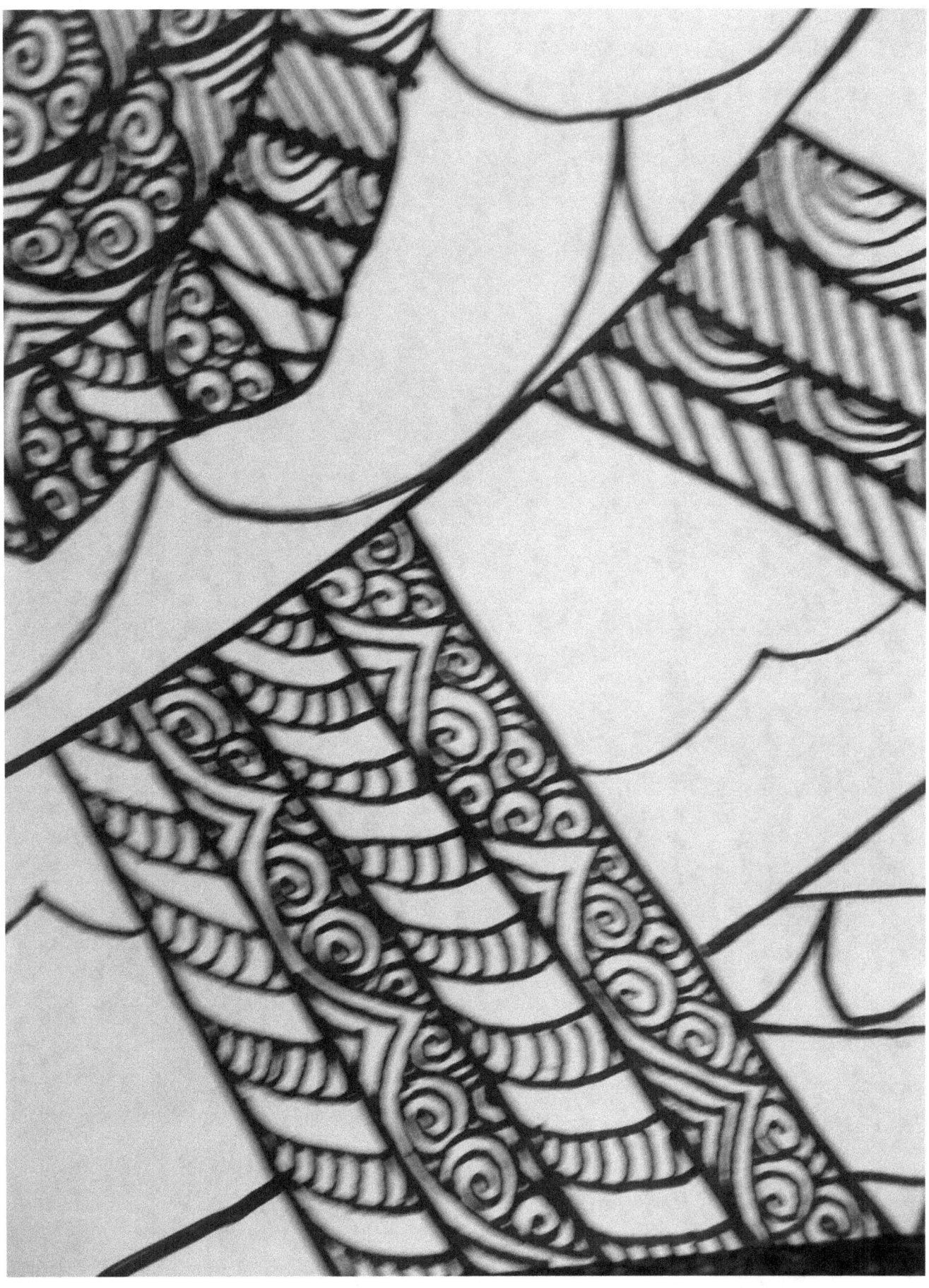

Bobby J. Jones

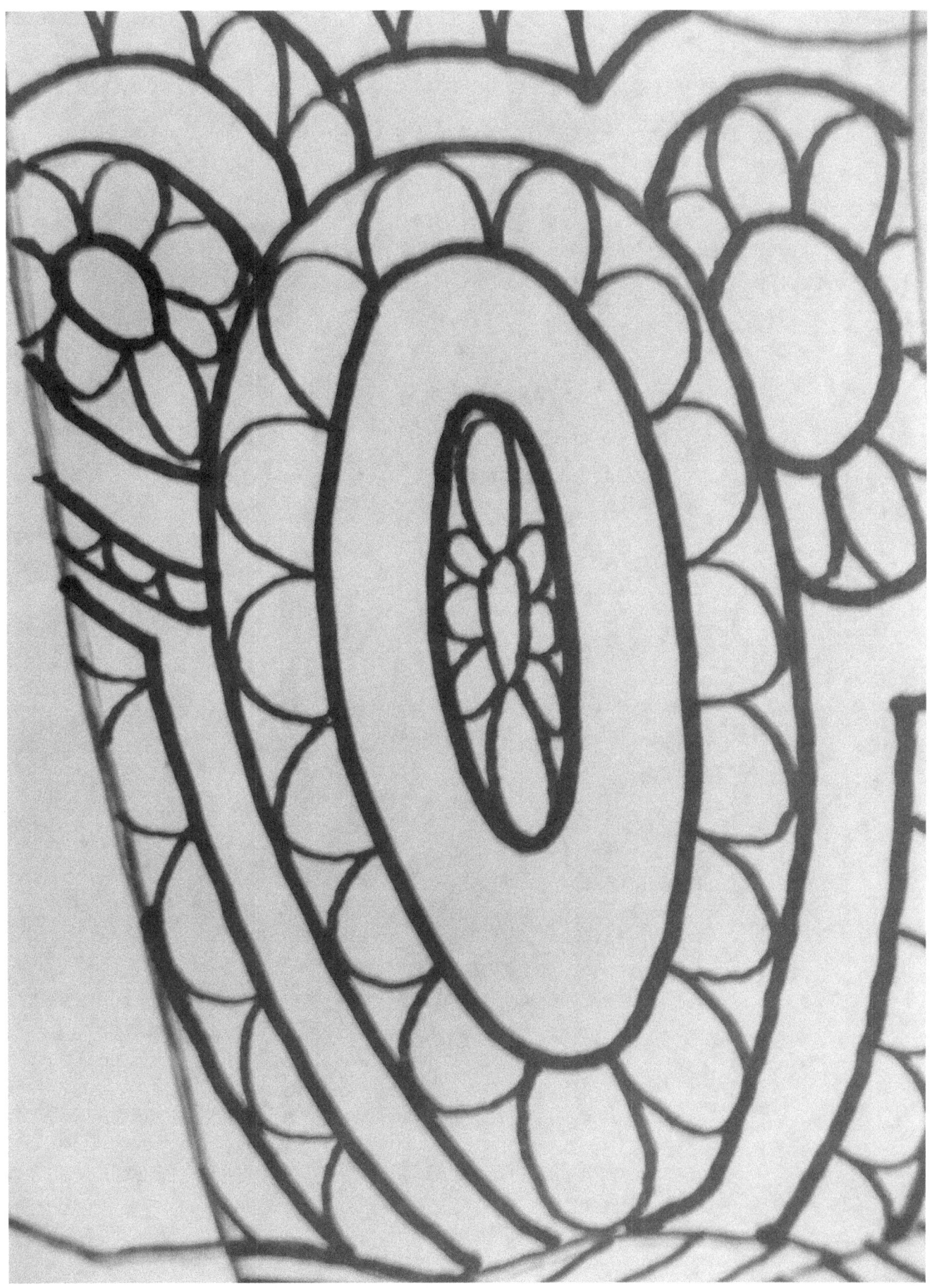

Bobby J. Jones

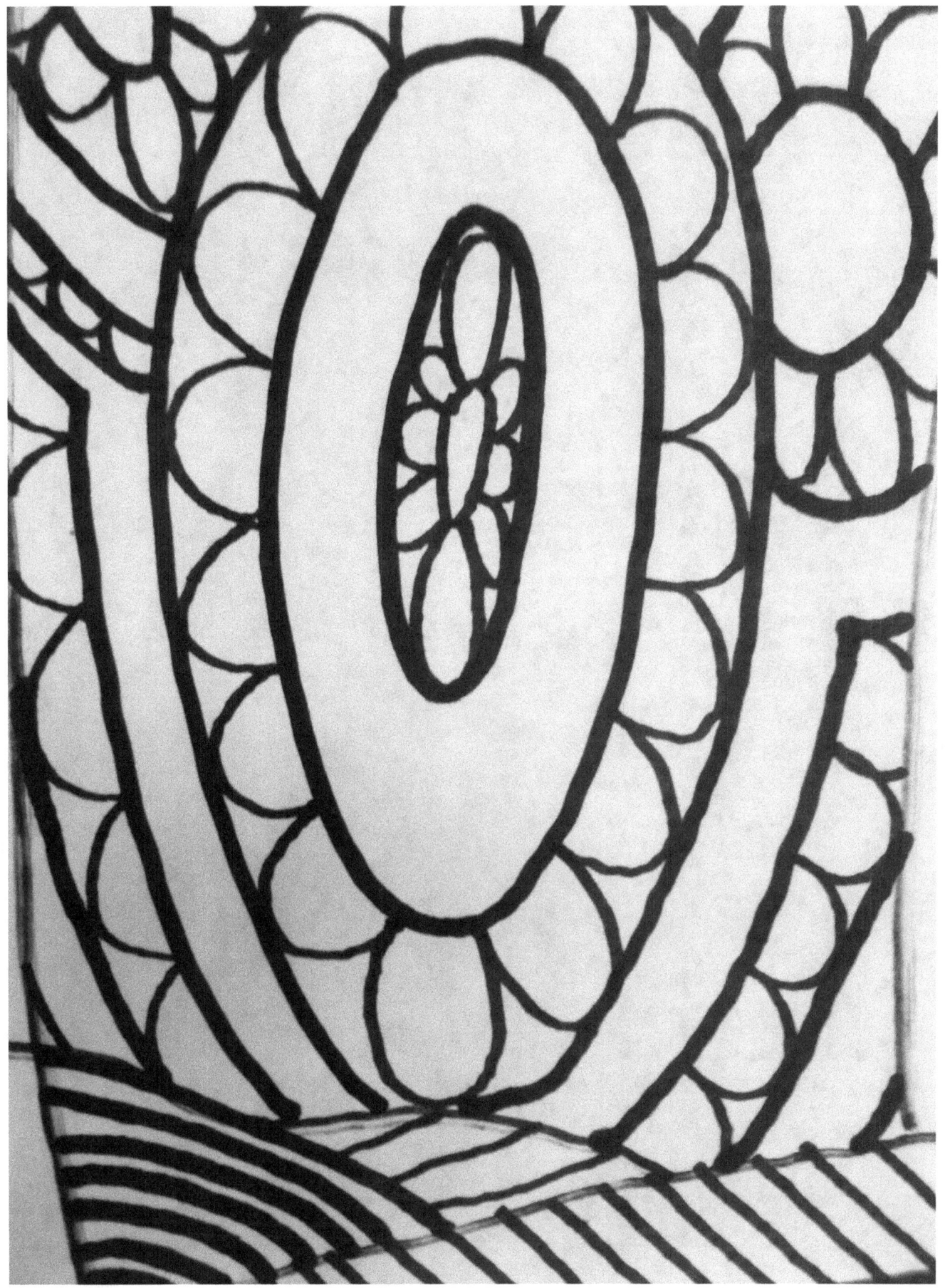

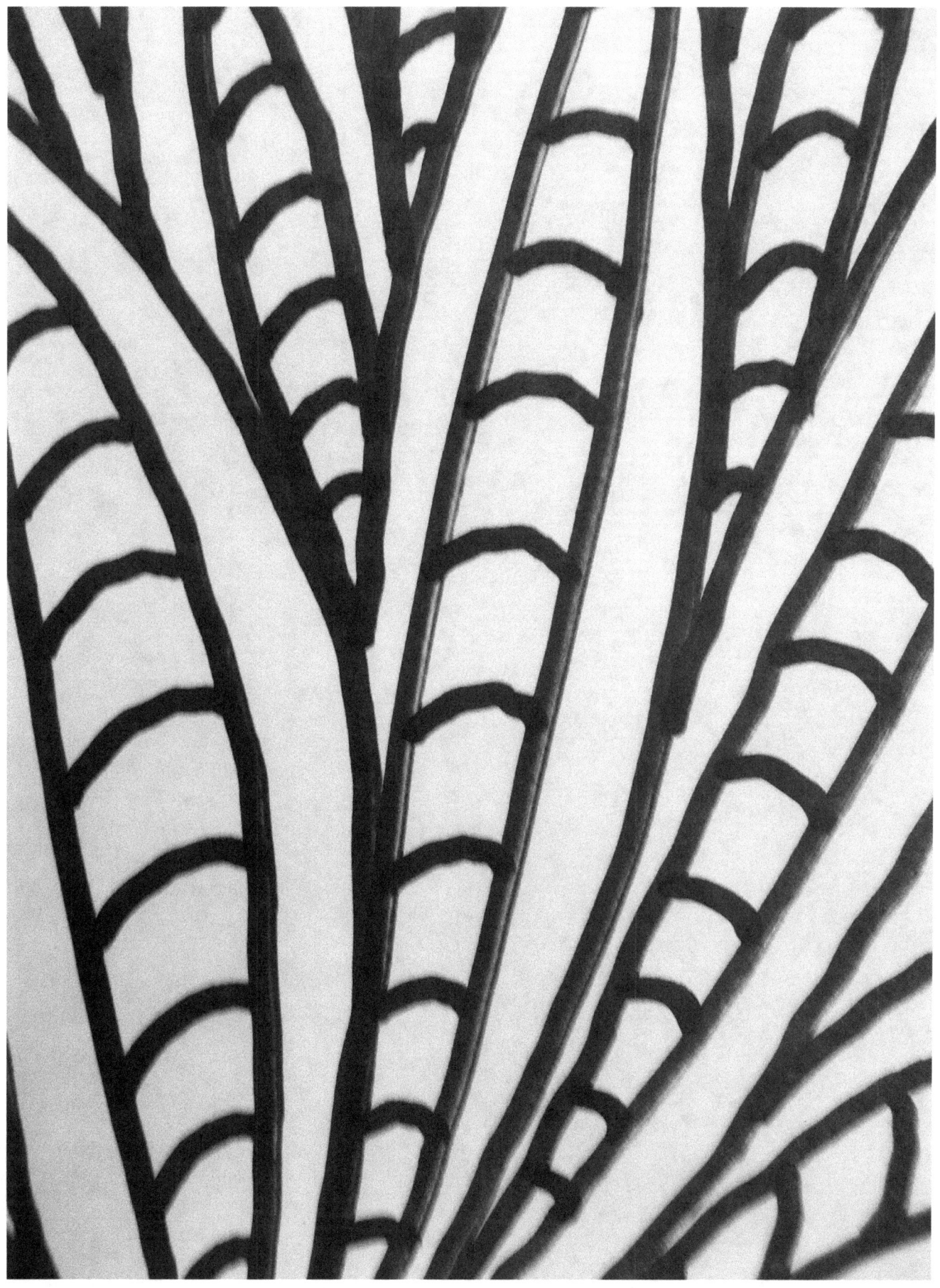

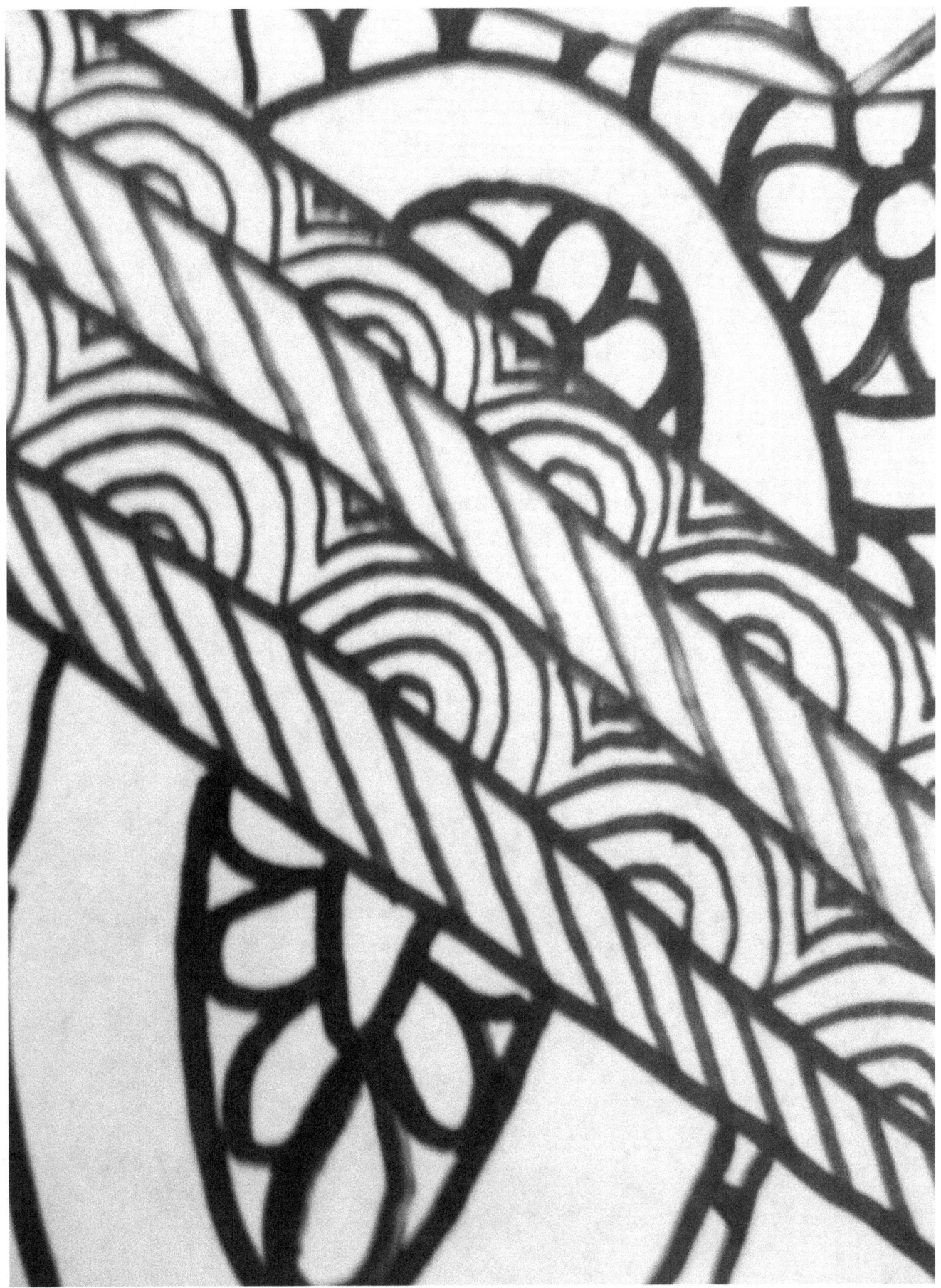

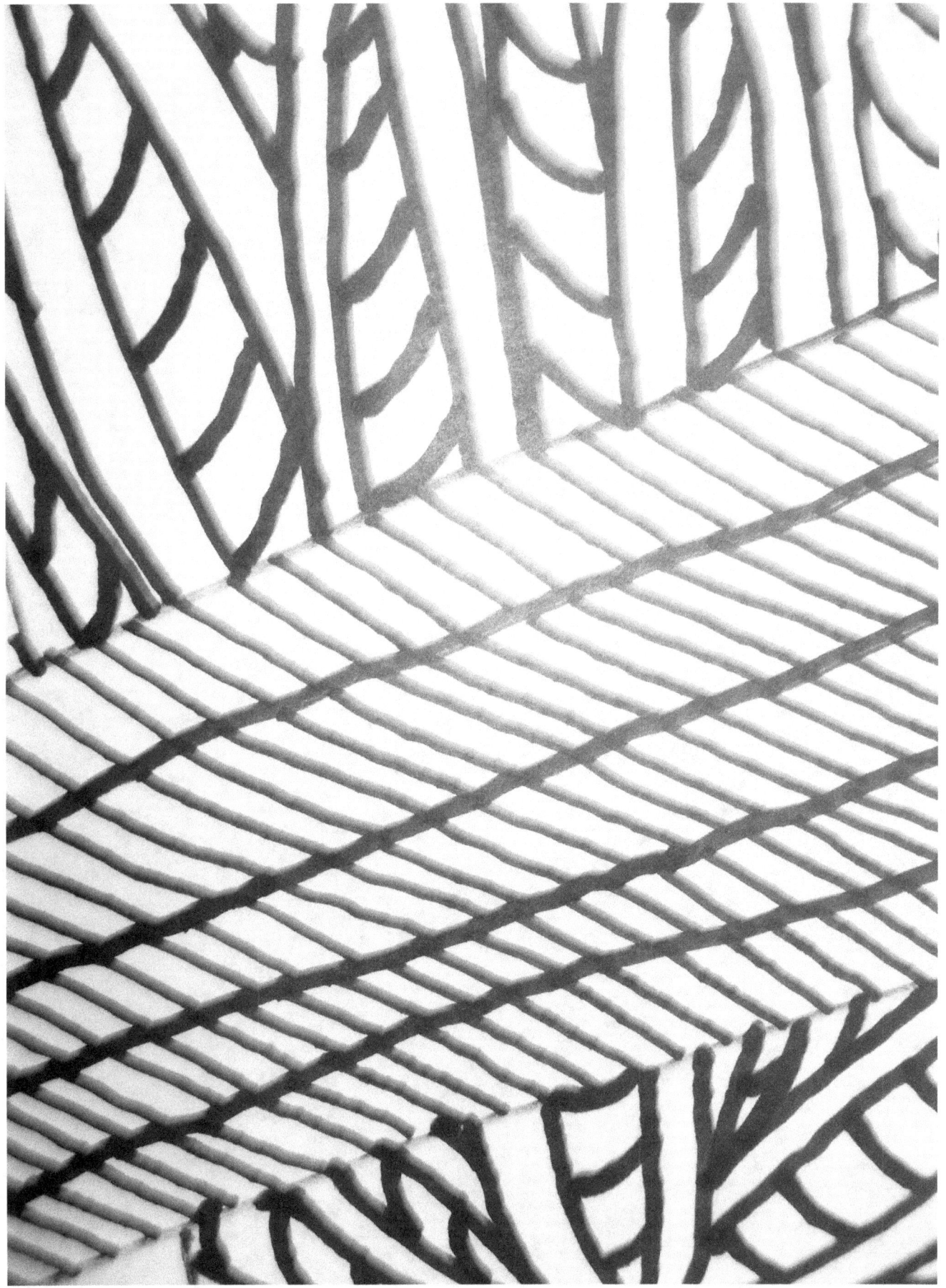

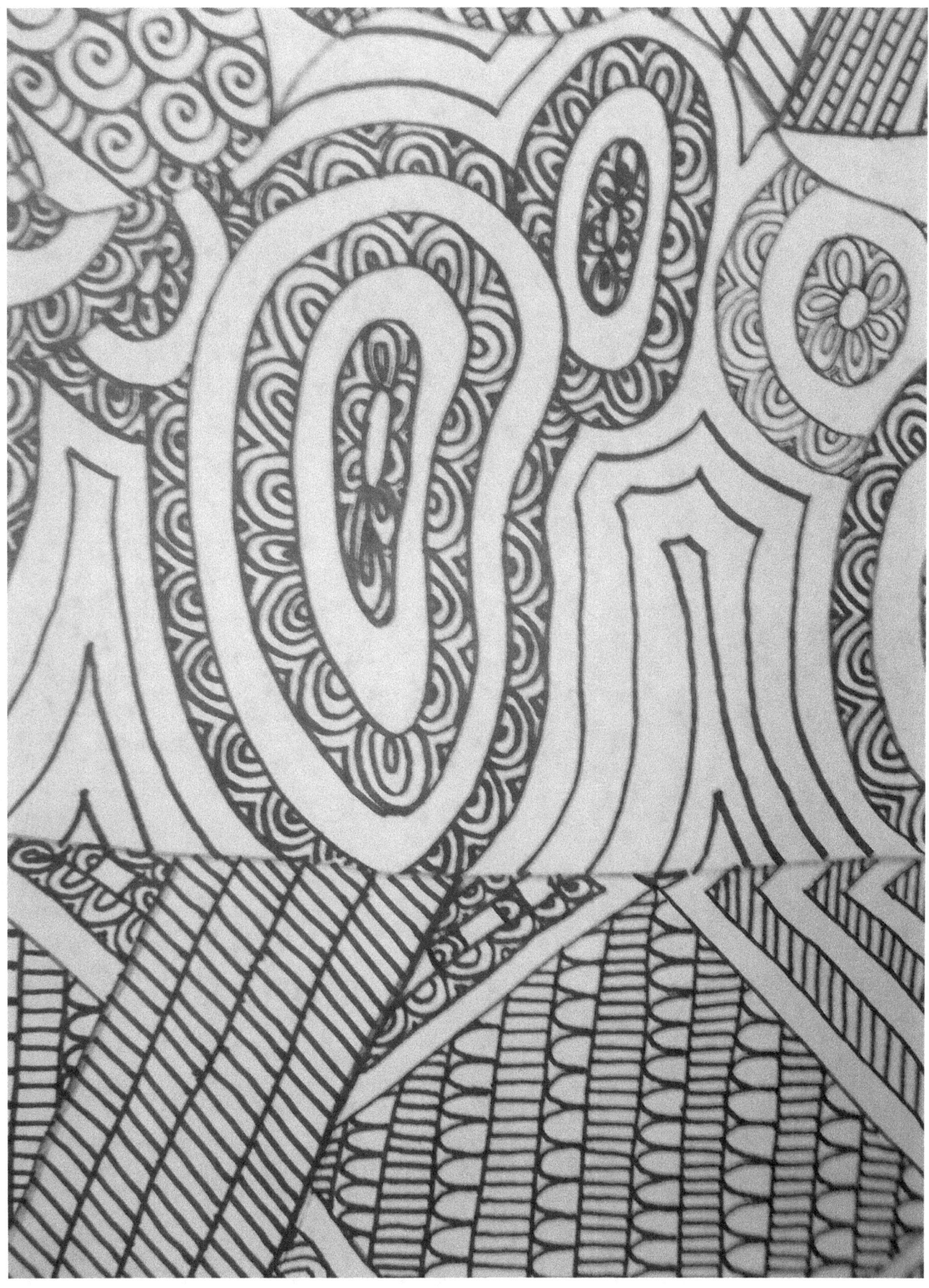

Bobby J. Jones

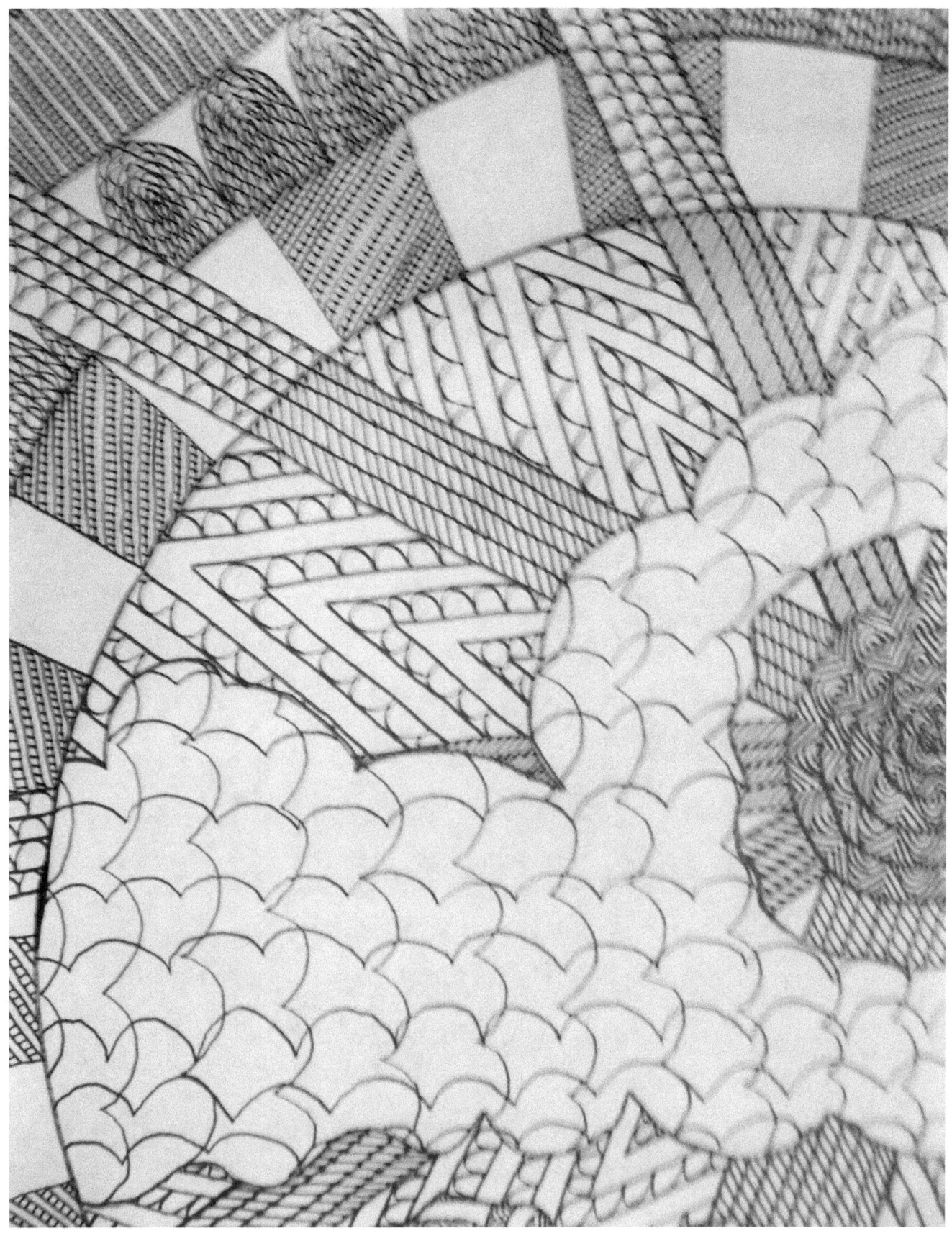

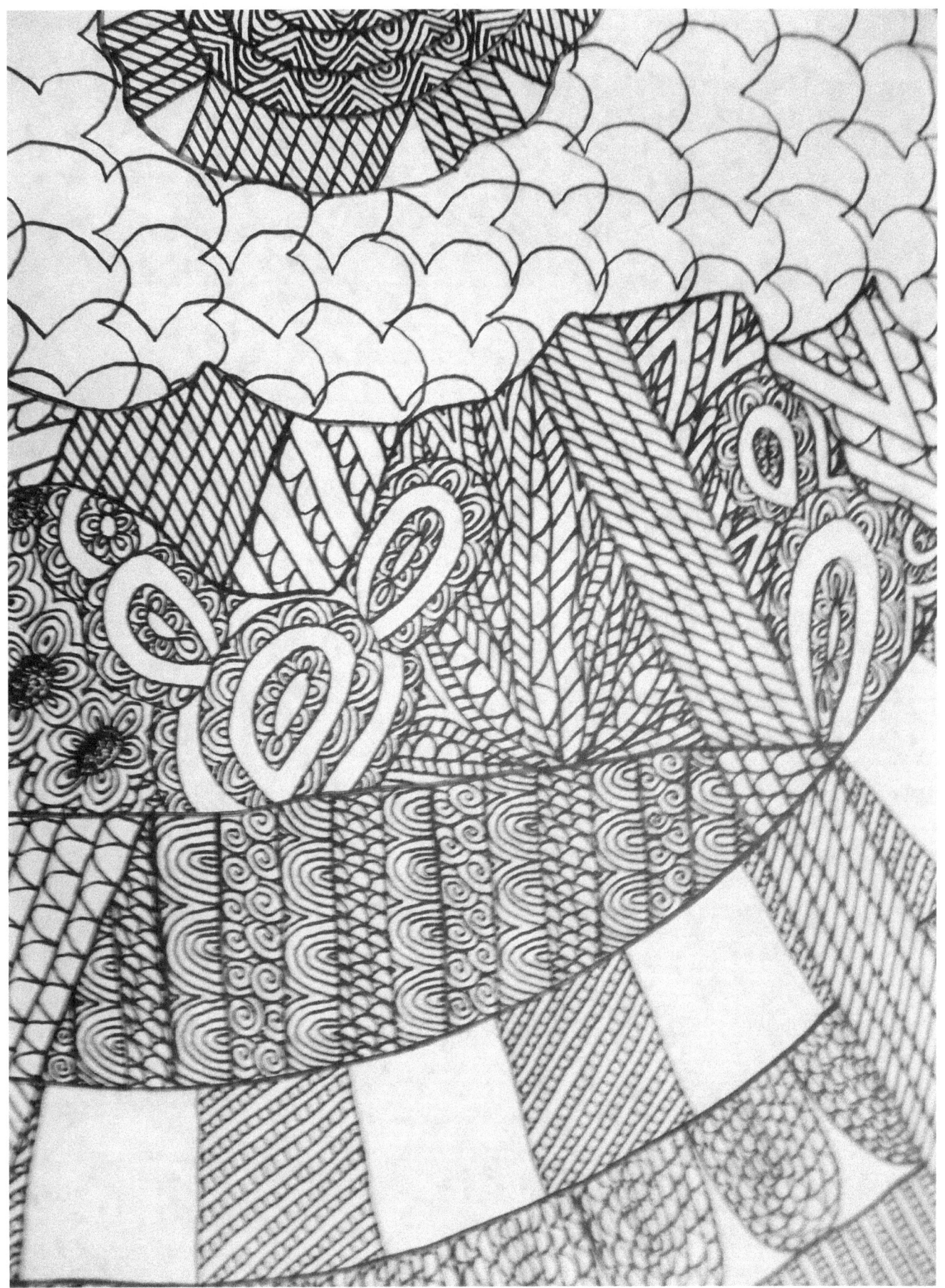

Bobby J. Jones

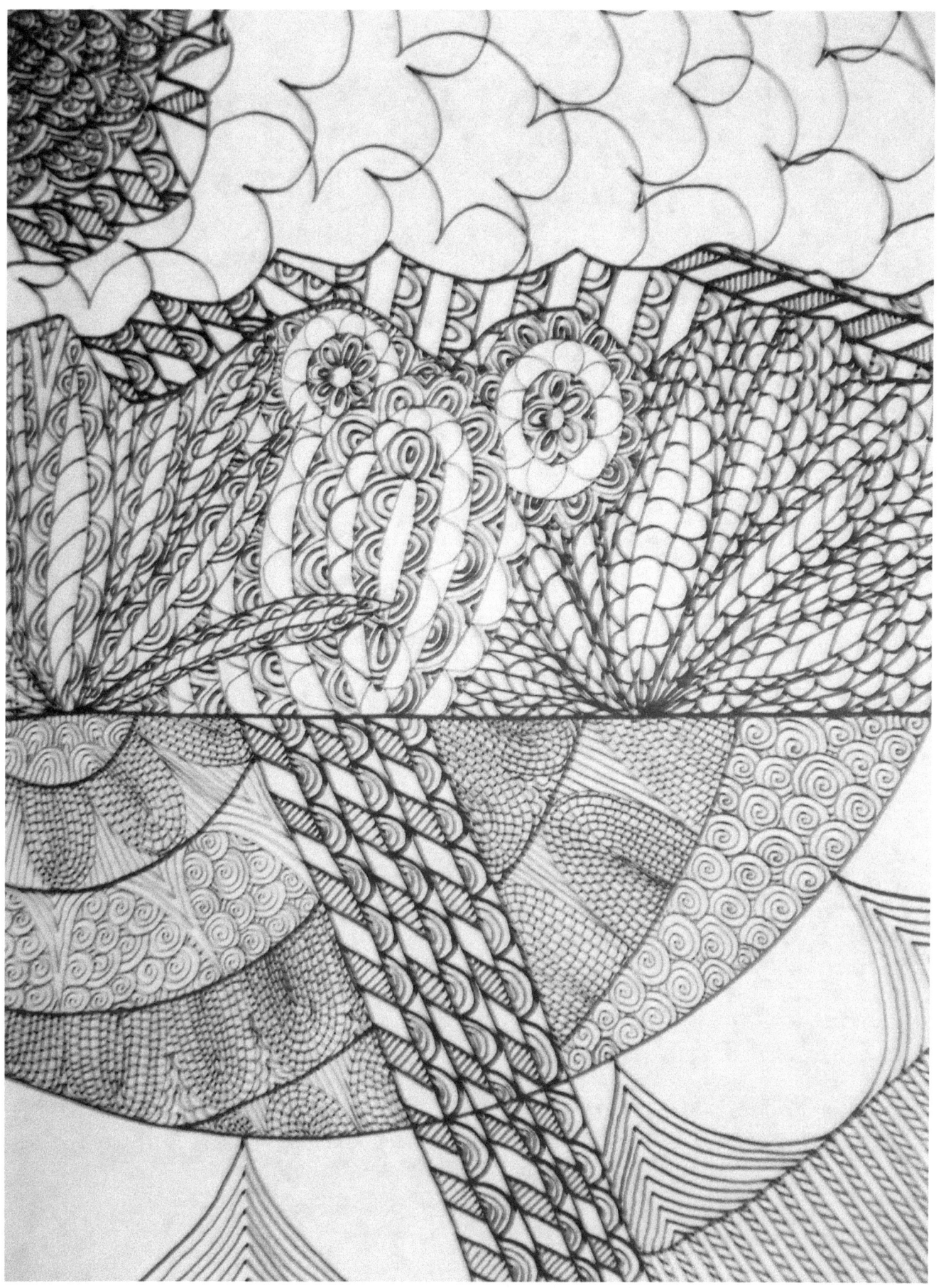

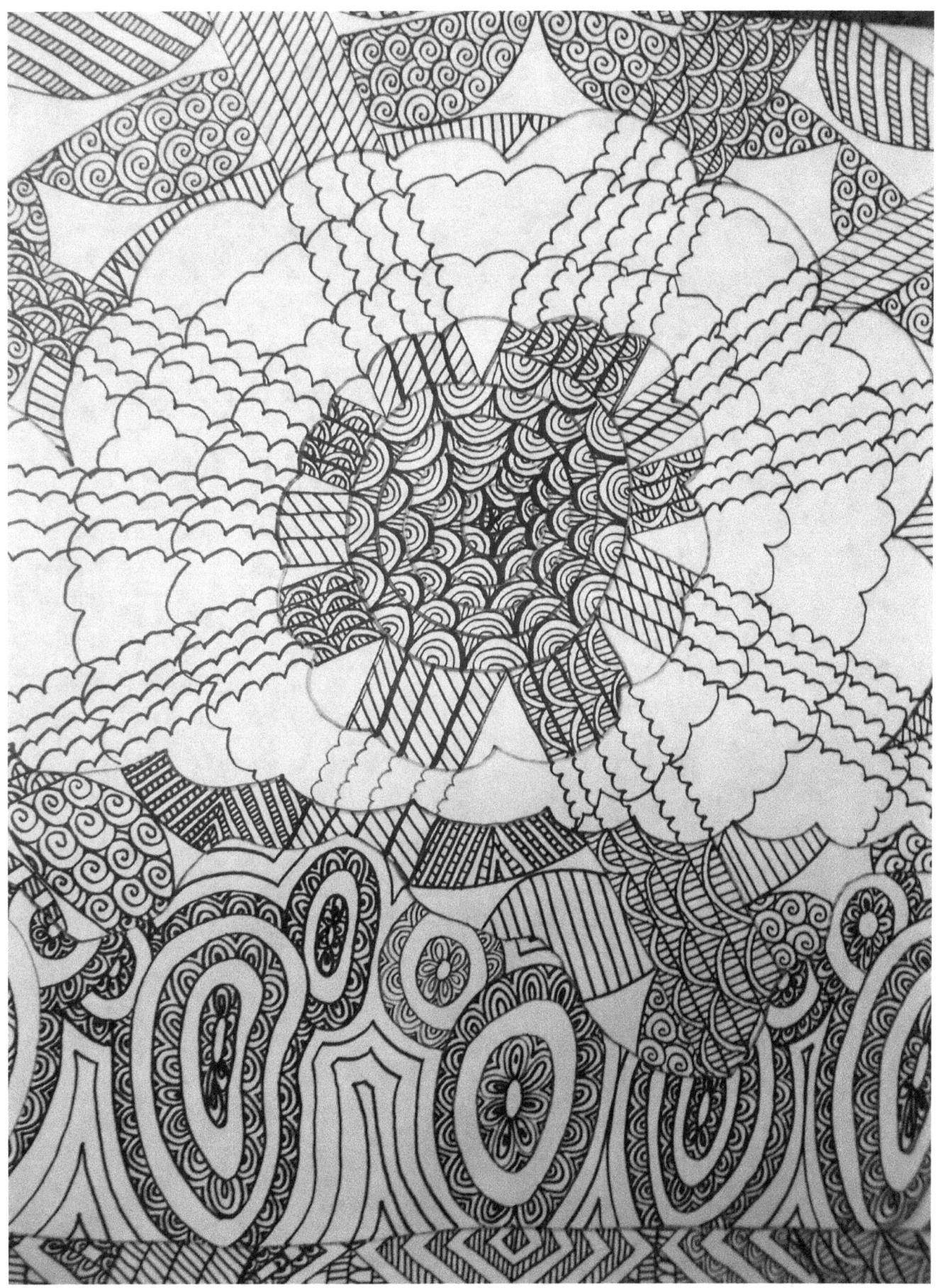

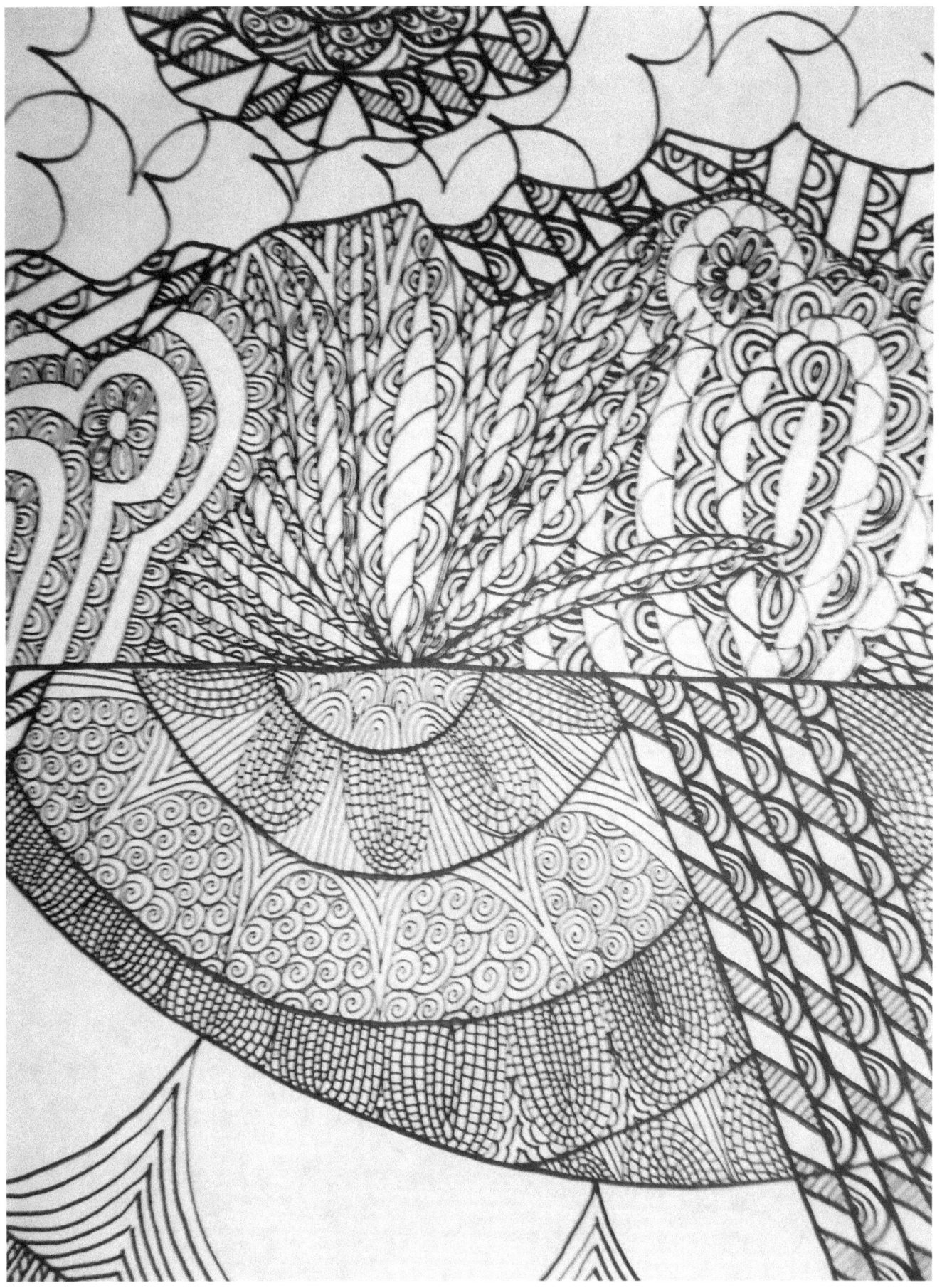

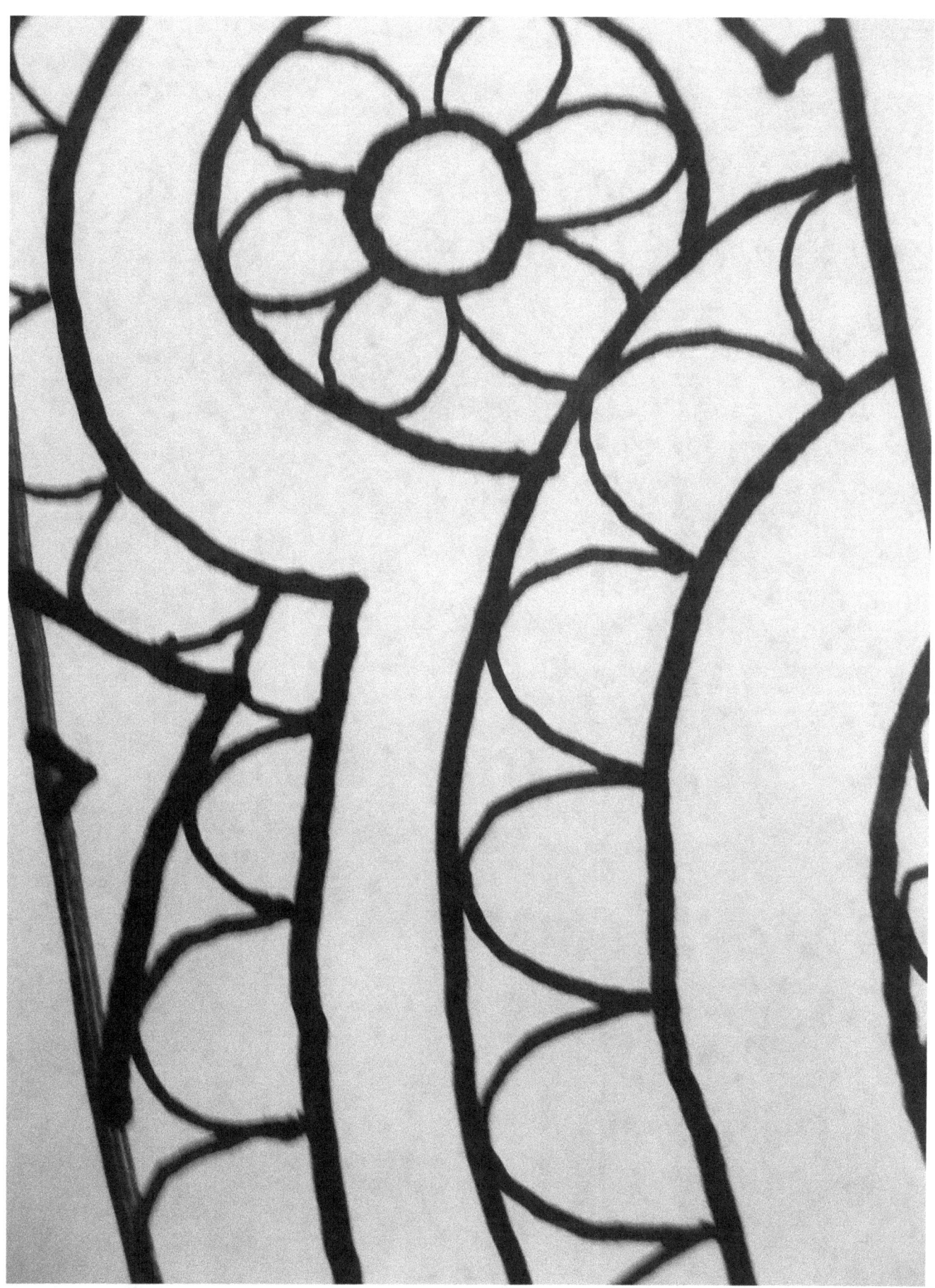

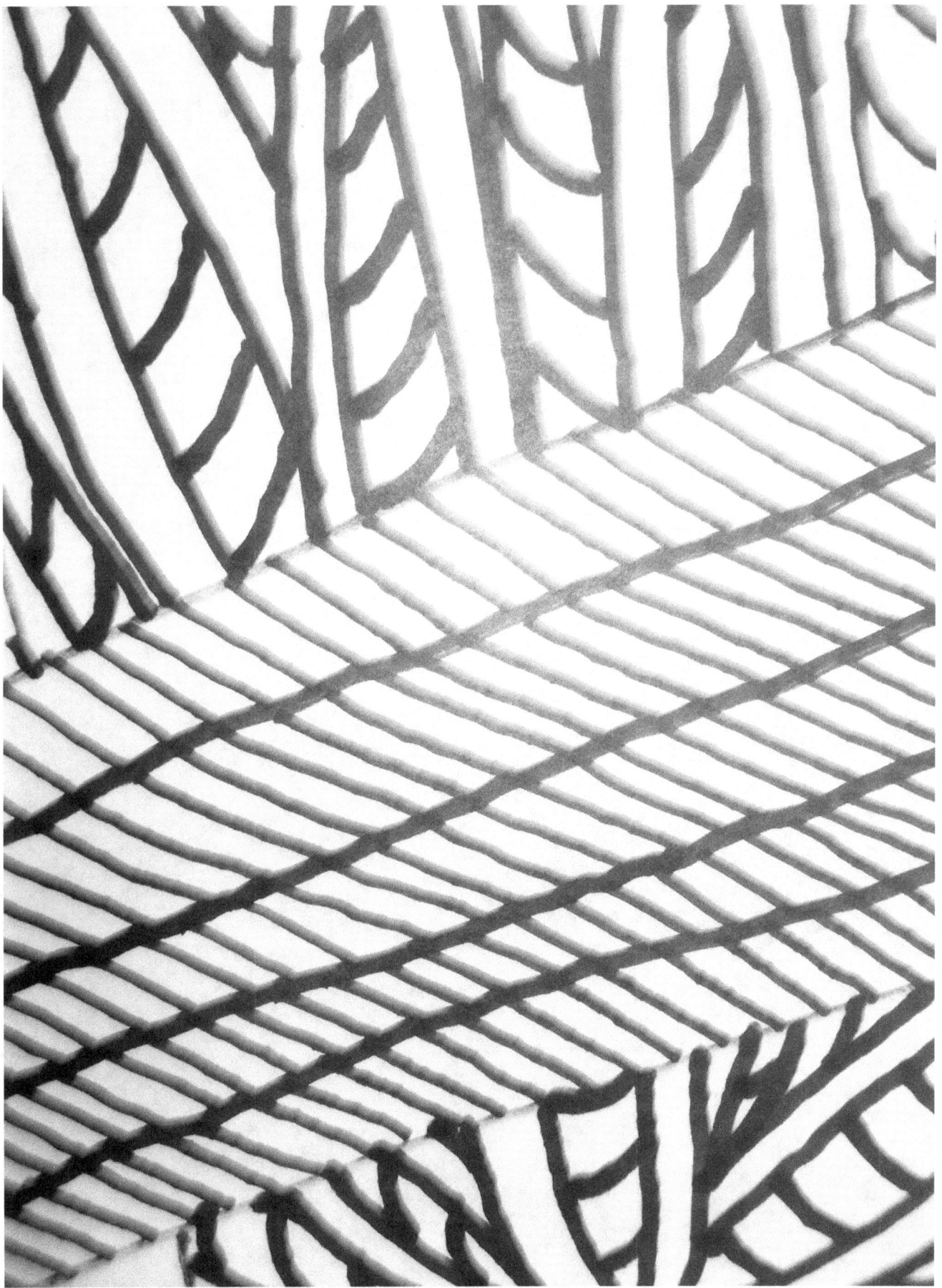

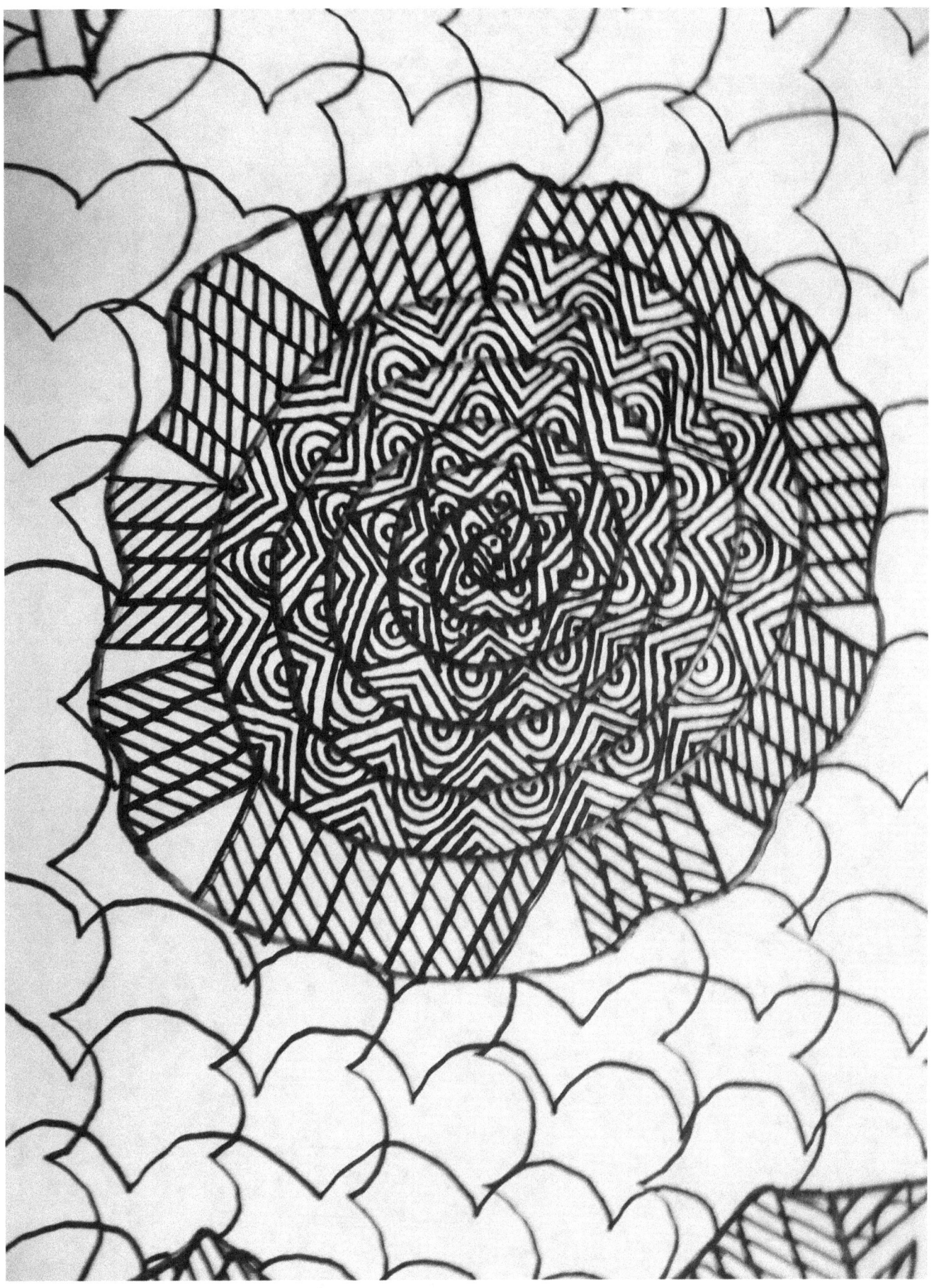

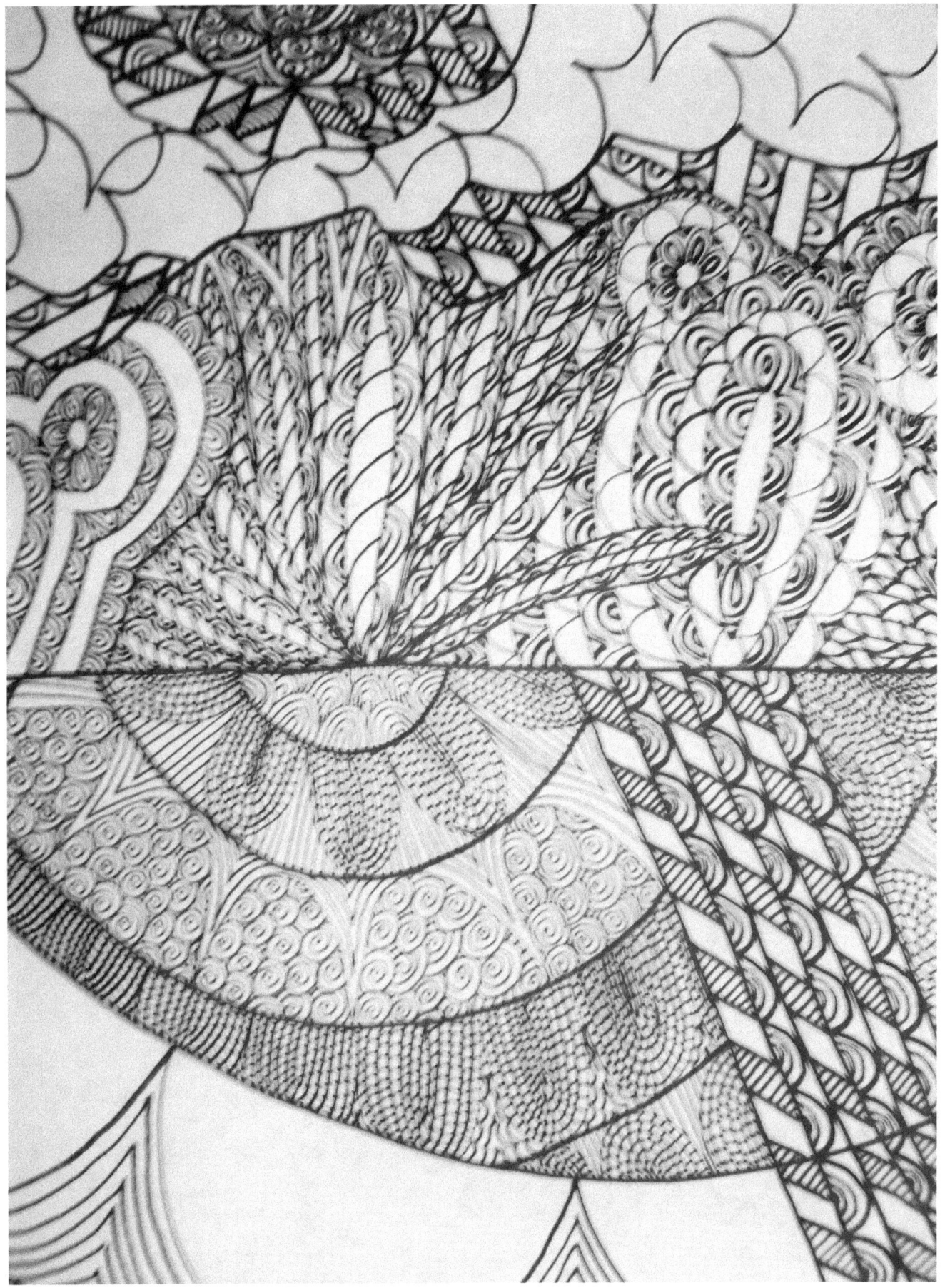

# About the Author

Bobby Jones was born at Reese Air Force Base in Lubbock, Texas in 1966. His family moved to Fort Worth, Texas in 1968. While growing up in Fort Worth, Texas, Jones attended school in The Fort Worth Independent School District. He graduated from Southwest High School in 1985 with honors.

Jones' father Toney Jones worked for General Dynamics as an Industrial Engineer for 25 years while Bobby's mother Kate Jones taught preschool for 20 years at Wedgwood Methodist Church, which became Genesis United Methodist Church in Fort Worth. Jones is the youngest son out of two daughters and two sons. He has two nieces, two nephews, and two great- grandnephews.

Jones attended Texas Tech University in Lubbock, Texas from 1985-1989. He received a BFA in Studio Art (Painting and Drawing) with honors in 1989. Bobby was a member of Alpha Phi Omega at Texas Tech and Golden Key. Then he attended The University of New Mexico in Albuquerque, NM. He obtained a Masters of Art in Art Education (Museum Education, Ceramics, and Photography) in 1994.

Bobby moved to Southern California in 1997 and worked in retail management from 1999 to 2009 for various retail companies in the Palm Springs area. Jones returned to New Mexico in 2009. He worked in the customer service profession from 2010 to 2014.

Jones attended Central New Mexico Community College. Bobby obtained an Alternative Teaching Degree in Special Education and was inducted into Phi Theta Kappa. He started working for Albuquerque Public Schools as a substitute teacher in Special Education.

He is currently an Educational Assistant in Special Education at Adobe Acres Elementary School in Albuquerque, New Mexico. Bobby accepted an offer with Lowe's Call Center, plans to advance with the company, and create his art. He is also a member of First Unitarian Church in Albuquerque.

Jones is also an artist and creates two dimensional mixed media art that consists of his painting and drawing skills. His artistic inspiration focuses upon the environment of New Mexico. He has exhibited his work at The Factory on 5th, The Tortuga Gallery, The 606 Gallery, and First Unitarian Church's Social Hall.

He is currently preparing for an art exhibit at The South Broadway Cultural Center in January and June, 2019. His art entry for The 28th ArtsThrive Exhibit was accepted by the art jury members. Three art pieces will be on display at The Albuquerque Museum starting October 19, 2018 in New Mexico. Jones will be featured in one of the collective art exhibits at The Tortuga Gallery in 2019 in Albuquerque, New Mexico.

His artwork appeared in The Desert Sun newspaper (Palm Springs, CA) in the special edition of the first year anniversary of 9/11 and the 40th anniversary of The Kennedy Assassination. Jones also created an art gallery on Facebook, Bobbo66Art Gallery. He invites everyone to look at his art creations.

The artist freehands these original images in this coloring book. Jones does not use computer software programs, rulers or t-squares to create these beautiful images. He enjoys seeing the imperfections in his work. The imperfections are what make Jones' work uniquely original. Jones suggests to the people that buy this book. They can doodle on the blank pages opposite the blackline images or create their own dreamscapes. He is creating a series of coloring books and is creating images for his next coloring book for children of all ages.